YEARS of PRAISE

An Authorized Autobiographical Sketch of

IRA SCATLIFFE

by

Dr. Joan B. Foster, Ph.D.

ISBN-10: 1533601623
ISBN-13: 978-1533601629

Published by Bell Publishing

Printed by CreateSpace, an Amazon.com company.
www.CreateSpace.com
Available from Amazon.com and other retail outlets.
Book design by Larry Smith
www.LarrySmithDesign.com

Foreword

There are many people in the Christian world who have strong music ability and who are able to play a musical instrument skillfully with precision. However, as coveted as musical creativity, techniques, and technical proficiency may be, they can never replace the anointed, life changing power of God.

Ira Scatliffe is one saxophonist who has held his own for the entirety of his musical career during which he has chosen to appear on the circuit of God's personal sound stage. With all of the technical skills and creativity required to master his chosen instrument, Ira's virtuosity is unrivaled. He has that rare gift that can only be masterfully created and uniquely designed –for it is an original designer masterpiece from God. This is not something to be argued – it is not given by man. It was created by God, for God and expressed through God's presence. Those who have sat under Ira's renditions and performances are first hand witnesses to the powerful anointing upon him as he yields both instrument and talent to serve the people of God. I have seen people healed, restored, and delivered. I have witnessed change in the atmosphere, attitude and in the unifying of a people through his music.

There is a familiar saying borrowed from Scripture concerning the musicians in the Church – that their talents and gifts are without repentance. This is no different in Ira's case. He just happens to take God's Word very seriously.

As long as I have known him, this has been Ira Scatliffe, my best friend's brother. We played together for some years at the Church of God of Prophecy in around the Washington DC metropolitan area. While I have expressly tinkered on the ivories and enjoyed playing the piano, Ira became established within the Christian community as a gifted saxophonist. His connections and affiliations have led to many engagements throughout the Church of God across the United States and Virgin Islands. His many years on the local circuit armed with his spiritual weapon have contributed to his view of the today's world as God has used him to help other ministries achieve their goals.

Humbly acknowledging his lifelong dedication to God, Ira has always admitted to being a true worshiper – not by accident, but by the divine call of God upon his life. Many years ago, He declared he would never take the gift given to him by God and use it for the enemy. On those rare occasions when I am blessed to see or speak with him, I am pleased to testify that Ira's declaration is the same. He opened his mouth to the Lord on this thing and he has not changed.

Martin Luther said beautiful music is the art of the prophets that can calm the agitations of the soul; it is one of the most magnificent and delightful presents God has given us and that next to the Word of God, the noble art of music is the greatest treasure in the world. Well, although Ira does play beautiful music, I would say that this is a woefully inadequate description of the presence of the Holy Spirit when He breathes upon this instrument of talent extraordinaire. You see, it is not so common today for musicians to surrender their gifts to permit the Holy Spirit the freedom to minister as He will through their instruments: that is, it is rare for a musician to release his own love of an instrument so that healing, miracles, prophecy – all of the gifts of the Spirit may flow to the people. Few understand that they are the instrument of the Lord. Too often, pride gets in the way.

However, a truly anointed musician understands that his ministry functions in a 3-fold capacity and extends beyond playing notes in the right order. Ira picks up his instrument for the joy of doing this. He listens to the inward leading of the Holy Spirit so that as he plays, he can then worship, minister and serve. Others are then able to receive and release the blessings of heaven as God pours into their lives through divine inspiration.

With the pride out of the picture, he has ability to create an atmosphere of praise and adoration. It is through this that Ira has become known for ushering us to another level of worship. We thank God for such a minister of music – still after all these years, he is still praising and worshiping God!

- *Dr. Joan Foster*
Calvary Christian College

Dedication

◆ ◆ ◆

To the loving memory of my parents
The late Edwin and Eurina Scatliffe
That God divinely placed in my life to
Bring me up in the admonition of the Lord.
That was one of the best gifts.

In honor of my dear sister
The late Naomi Scatliffe Donaldson
She will always be in my heart.

To my loving sister Ruth and my brother Ulric
For looking out for me and
Who always cheers me onward.

To my beautiful daughter, Jyrah
My God given treasure.

To my loving wife, Julie
The light of my life who is always with me and
Wrapped around my heart for eternity.

"If I could be anywhere in the world –
If I could be doing anything I wanted –
I would be playing the saxophone
in Europe and all around the world
for Jesus.
For it is in Him
that I have my being."

Ira Scatliffe

Preface

When I began the initial work on Forty Years of Praise, the intent was to present a single collection of music inspired by memories of the days gone by when I spent night after night on my knees before God seeking His face. Years ago, the Lord sought me out individually for this time of life. I am convinced that each of us is an important part of God's plan.

Imagine that, the infallible, all powerful God, caring about one child sitting on a lonely bleacher holding his saxophone. This wonderful Savior, my deliverer, keeper and strong tower, visited with me back in the U.S. Virgin Islands and in a moment, the twinkling of an eye, my sixth grade troubles went away.

Who is this God that cares so much to the extent that He would give His only begotten Son to the cause of humanity but even after that sacrifice with Jesus Christ dying on the cross in our place, He would still stop in for a visit to encourage me? His humanistic qualities – Jesus went through pain and suffering, rejection and humiliation – made Him relatable. It still stirs deep within my heart, that He cared enough about my elementary school boy issues to take a personal interest in my life.

God intricately designed and structured the human body with its three trillion cells and its DNA, deoxyribonucleic acid, the hereditary material found in humans. But still He was not done. One day, He put into motion His grand plan just for me. What plan? He instilled within me the love of Christ and gave me the heavenly gift of music. It is one of the rare gifts that transcends the barriers of language, creed, and race.

It is His love that inspires Christians to come together for the purpose of making the world a better place. God will do everything within His power to draw man to Himself. The gift of music that He gave me is not just for me alone. It is to bless God and His people. While we cannot comprehend everything, we do know that His unconditional love is matchless and works wonders. It is the mystery of His grace. There is no greater love. I am a living witness.

Acknowledgments

My indebtedness goes back to very early times and begins with all of the teachers, pastors and educators at various levels throughout all aspects of my life. From the beginning until now, the startling fact is, they have been influential on many levels throughout my life. In a most unusual but providential way, they have been with me from the time I was a teenager until this day, lifting me up and encouraging me to go forth.

For all of the work that has gone into the creation of this book and for many prayers of the saints. I give God praise. With special honor to God for the call upon my life, and express thanks to my pastor, who prayed and encouraged me when I first began this journey, though it seems inadequate. My dad saw in me the potential for success. His insistence, to go all the way, spawned the beginning of this work. Something he said, "You are gifted, son" has remained with me throughout the creation of this book for it is a reminder that God put us together. He was my best friend. It is not enough to simply play the saxophone but I am persuaded that this is the call of God on my life. I must play the saxophone relentlessly! For a variety of other forms of help and encouragement, I acknowledge the Church of God of Prophecy pastors, bishops and lay-ministers who stood by me through these 40 years of praise.

My utmost acknowledgment goes to my invisible literary supporter, Dr. Joan Foster, who labored, not to make her own voice heard, but to enable others to hear my voice through my personal experiences and beyond those accounts in order that my story might be told. It is through her that the dream of writing my memoirs materialized and developed into reality. Her insightfulness, comprehension and special knack for understanding what I really wanted to say, has made it possible to convey my message. For this, I am grateful.

My most precious acknowledgment goes to my daughter who puts a lot of love into everything she does. Hearing her play saxophone is the joy of my life. I cannot express enough love for my wife Julie, who assisted me in many ways in preparing for this book. For her patience, love and many hours of cheering me on throughout this project, I give my neverending, undying love.

Introduction

Praise – the most unselfish act possible of ministering to God while in the midst of pain.

-Borrowed from Kim Clement

It is impossible to begin the story of my journey without some mention of the title of this book because it has been some 40 years that I have been traveling down this road. A lot has happened in what seems to be a relatively short time. To me, the whole world has changed and yet, I remain in a certain state, my eyes fixed toward heaven. As is common when reaching a certain plateau in your life, a whole lot of clichés and adages come to mind. For instance, we have heard sayings like "Life begins at forty" or "Once you reach 40, its downhill after that." W. B. Pitkin's sayings may be right for some folks but not necessarily for God's people. However, most people do agree that 40 years is a major milestone and it is sufficient for a person to have collected enough life experience to have something wise to say. One thing's for sure: If all goes well and if you live long enough, you will reach a 40 year landmark someday.

Regardless of whether it is related to age or some profound perspective on life, 40 years is a time when people begin to evaluate or assess their lives. They make comparisons, look for patterns, make iconic parallels, and constantly try to shape how to view those years.

Though *Forty Years of Praise* is actually not about turning 40, one might say that for the last four decades, I have scaled the precipice of a period of my life in which these precious years have culminated in a data bank of lessons drawn from the past. The good news is that I was not spending those years chasing frivolous dreams, worrying about accumulating wealth or entertaining the world. My focus was entirely different. This is how *Forty Years of Praise* began.

When I was a kid, I would ride along with my mom and my dad who would be engaged in a heavy conversation. My mind would drift far off into the future. Sometimes I would hang out with my friends, playing softball or something. While they were talking or kidding around, I often found my thoughts wandering off someplace else. Even though I was just a kid, there was something buried deep within my spirit and I wanted to do more than simply exist. Back then, I knew that there must be more to life. I have seen the inscription of many epitaphs – *"They were born and they died"*. There was nothing in between. I wanted to live that "in between". I wanted to do something with my life! At the center of it was a desire to please God. But I never spoke of it to anyone. I did not know how to put those thoughts into words and it wasn't proper dinner table talk. Besides, who would be responsible for making it happen besides the Lord? If you are born again, and the Holy Spirit is abiding in you, He will communicate with you through your Spirit. He makes plans for you starting early in your life. So this was between just the two of us. If I was down home, I would say – it was just between me and the Lord.

You see, while on this pilgrimage, if you will, I went through a lot. We all have our own testimonies. Young and old people alike, we all have a cross to bear or something that we have to endure. I have encountered many mighty men of God and have seen great men fall by the wayside or give up on this journey. However, I am still praising God and determined to stand for righteousness despite the odds mounted against me. For some 40 years, I have faced rejection, lived through cultural prejudices, fought back many tears, and battled through my fears. If not for God, I would not be here. Because of Him, I have witnessed miracles. I have seen lowly men rise up in the power of the Lord's might. Despite all odds they walked out from under the oppression because of the anointing.

At different times, I have paralleled the lives of Biblical figures and studied their timelines in an attempt to understand more about this period in my life. What is this great number, the number 40 – that registers so profoundly throughout the living Word of God and what has it to do with me? I am not alone with this number. Nor am I the first person that has come to this place. Other believers recognize the move of God on their lives and understand the value of what God is speaking and doing. Conservative scholars remain cautious about assigning too much importance to numbers in the Bible, as this has lead some groups to mystical and theological extremes, believing numbers can reveal the future, or uncover hidden information which can lead to delving into the dangerous realm of divination. However, certain prophetic books of the Bible, such as Daniel and Revelation, introduce a complex, interrelated system of numerology which exhibits definite patterns.

The number 40 is all over the Bible and traditionally, most Bible scholars agree that it does possess some symbolic or literal significance relevant to the period of testing, trial or probation of any kind and that it denotes completion or fulfillment. It usually represents a period when times are hard and a person's faith is tested. We know the story of the Israelites who wandered in the Wilderness of "Sin", which is the Hebrew word for the Sumerian moon god, from which "Sinai" is derived, for 40 years as punishment for their "stiff-necked unbelief." Elijah spent 40 days on the same mountain worshiping God. The most notable are the 40 days and nights of rainfall associated with the Flood of Noah when the whole world flooded to a depth of some 15 feet above the tallest mountains. Moses lived 40 years in Egypt and 40 years in the desert before God selected him to lead his people out of slavery. It is just as significant that he was also on Mount Sinai for 40 days and nights, on two separate occasions, receiving God's laws. We can even look at Jesus who fasted for 40 days in the wilderness before being tempted by Satan and this was during the 40 days and nights of fasting just before his ministry began.

Though everybody has a story to tell, and though it never occurred to me until now that I might have one, I am a living witness that God has given me a life of purpose filled with prayer and praise. It is only because of His anointing and by His grace, that I am still walking out this testimony. For these 40 years, through thick and thin; and with the odds stacked against me, I have trusted God. A lot has happened during this period. Society has changed. The mindset of the people in Christendom has been altered. The whole world is very different, transformed by the digital revolution and advances in medicine and human knowledge. It seems as if the earth has begun to fall off her axis and everything has sped up exponentially as man struggling to survive self-made pitfalls. We must pray lest even the very elect, is turned upside down.

Now that the years have passed and I am blessed with my own family, I can see how God's plan for my life has shaped me. All that I am and ever hope to be, is totally wrapped up in Him and sealed under the protection of the divine Holy Spirit.

If we check ourselves individually, we might discover that we are each on a journey. I am consciously walking out my legacy even as we move forward in this discussion. My trust is that God, who is well able, who has shaped, molded, and preserved me, will propel me further to the next place and on to the next thing. There have been times when people would try to persuade me to go in a different direction but I belong to God and will function in the call on my life that only comes from Him. He is my God and we, (my family and I) are His people.

The number 40 can also represent a generation of man. Because of their sins after leaving Egypt, God declared that the generation of Israelites who left Egyptian bondage would not enter their inheritance in Canaan so they wandered in the wilderness for 40 years before a new generation was allowed to possess the Promised Land.

It is not simply coincidence that the number 40 is mentioned 146 times throughout both Testaments. There is general consensus that the Bible seems to use numbers in patterns or to teach a spiritual truth. Other numbers are repeated in the Bible as well that give us pause for consideration as well but God does not call us to search for secret meanings, hidden messages, and codes in the Bible. There is more than enough truth in the words and meanings of Scripture to meet all our needs and make us "complete and thoroughly equipped for every good work" *(2 Timothy 3:16)*.

It is amazing to me that Jesus was tempted for 40 days and after the period ended, He showed up announcing that He was anointed to preach the gospel to the poor, to heal the broken hearted to preach deliverance to the captives and set at liberty those who were bruised.

At some point in all of our lives, we too, must come to that day. Personally, despite all that I have seen, done or the life I have lived, there came a time when I had to come to myself so after these particular 40 years, I am on my face before the Lord.

Now, do I really need to dwell on the significance of the 40 years? Not really, but I will share my story. It just might bless someone. We might all wake up to its significance in our own lives!

It is God who has made me. My feet are on solid ground. I yearn that they would be planted on higher ground and that I would possess all that God has for me. "Now oh Lord, if I have pleased you, what more will you have me do?"

We are here to occupy until He comes, yes, but there is much work to be done. The harvest is plentiful and the laborers are few. My heart spills over the altar before the Lord. Men ought to always pray. These are the words of my heart to the Lord. "Lord, these 40 years you have given me. You have been with me; you have blessed and kept me; and you have made me all that I am. And yet I stand here, all the more. May Your will be done in my life here now and forever."

Why now? Why such a stirring? It is clearly something that only God knows. I did not wake up one morning and simply declare "it has been 40 years and now I have something to say or do." It is only by the inward leading of the Holy Spirit that I deliver this message of praise and tell my story.

Chapter 1
Your Gift is Directly from God

Your talent is God's gift to you. What you do with it is your gift back to God.

-Leo Buscaglia

If you're one of God's children, you have been given the most awesome gift ever: grace. Through Jesus Christ we have eternal life and we have done nothing to deserve it. Even so, sometimes, we do not always understand or appreciate the gift. Never quite realizing its value, we often miss the whole point of the gift.

The perfect gift. A friend explained that once upon a time they wanted to give their twin sons what they thought were the "perfect" gifts so they would know how to show appreciation. The boys would always rip open the packaging, pull out their gifts, and then within minutes, their attention had moved on to something else. It drove my friends crazy. It happened every year – didn't matter what holiday. That next Christmas they decided they were going to find the ultimate gift that the boys had been raving about for months. They shopped and shopped; they searched and searched until they found the right gift. So then the day and moment came when the gifts would come out from under the tree. Everybody was so excited. The boys were about to unwrap their presents. The parents pulled out their cameras. They could not wait to see the boys' expressions. Well, the first one ripped open his gift like any little boy would and, sure enough, he pulled out the toy and began to play with it. The second one did the same. My friends felt great; they had managed to get the right gifts at last! They caught each other's satisfied glances and headed off to the kitchen to get something to drink. They returned after a few minutes and what did they see? One child was sitting in the box; the other one was jumping in and sliding across the floor in his box. They couldn't believe it – the gifts had been shoved away over in a corner someplace. Yet the boys ran about freely, dragging and kicking the boxes. Soon the parents caught on and were laughing merrily, too. Now they understood what the real gift was.

Talents and gifts. There is a difference between natural talents and supernatural gifts. A talent is natural, consisting of natural endowments, inherited from one's parents, received at birth. Many people who are not born again are very talented (they have artistic, musical, athletic, or mathematical ability, etc.). Talents come through the genes of natural inheritance; whereas supernatural gifts are directly from the Lord. Talent comes from the first Adam and, however attractive, is still a part of man's fallen nature. The gift is by the Holy Spirit, as it pleases Him.

I can remember staring out of the window and watching a little bird hop by on the window sill of my third grade class. To me, it did not appear to have much purpose for being there. As it crept closer and closer toward me, I remained perfectly still, barely breathing. Then, all of a sudden as it neared my hand, it swooped down catching a worm in its little beak before it took off soaring away from the window. I watched as it rose higher in the clear blue skies away from the noisy classroom, away from my wondering eyes and far away from me. It flew off into the bright blue yonder with barely a flutter of its wing. Just like that it was gone. And yet, only moments before, it was perched on window sill, just out of harm's way, grabbing a bite to eat. That was a good day. First, because I had just witnessed the beauty of God's handiwork. Secondly, because Mrs. Bradhurst, my third grade teacher (unlike my second grade teacher, Mrs. Brathwait, who absolutely loved me and took a lot of interest in me) did not catch me staring out of the window. She was an excellent teacher, but oh man, she was also very tough. Therefore, for a little while that day, I was able to dream that I would be just as free as that little sparrow. I thought of its freedom as a gift.

The real gift. But we also have to understand what the real gift is. Some people just don't understand gifts. As God gives unearned gifts among us in unequal measures, it has the effect of drawing into the light and exposing pride from the murky darkness of our deceptive hearts. This exposure of pride was all a part of God's design in the distribution of gifts among us. Every time we compare ourselves to others and either feel superior, inferior or resentful, it is God's way of inviting us to glorify him by repenting of our pride and humbling ourselves under his mighty, wise hand and trusting him to exalt us in due time as it pleases Him.

Strategic gifting. God established a two-way channel of blessing if we will embrace it. He strategically gifts us in such a way that our gifts channel blessings to others by meeting various needs. They channel the blessing of humility to us by exposing our pride and pushing us to receive God's grace to live by God-pleasing faith. When this happens it produces gratitude in everyone. It's perfect! Our gifts work together to bless others and sanctify us.

A talented person may be considered or recognized as outstanding. However, for full effectiveness talents need to be developed. In other words, a person who is naturally skilled musically must still learn to play an instrument, often demanding years of practice. Most professional athletes not only have natural talent but they have developed this talent through years of practice and hard work. Talents possessed by believers should be surrendered and consecrated to the Lord and used for His honor and glory.

Supernatural gifts. Gifts are supernatural, received from God. Though a person who is not born again might mimic a spiritual gift, it is counterfeit and limited to self-gratification or promotion (like a false prophet, a false teacher). Spiritual gifts are determined by God, not by natural talents which a man may possess. The gift that comes from God is far more rewarding and distinct from any natural teaching talent. When we are born again, He gives us a gift. Gifts need to be exercised and this can only happen as the believer stays spiritually healthy and grows in the grace and knowledge of the Lord Jesus Christ. The proper exercise of spiritual gifts requires spiritual growth and maturity. Gifts are given by God for the outworking of God's life as expressed by the Body of Christ. When the Body is healthy there is a corresponding manifestation of God glorified.

Despite any debates and confusion about supernatural gifts, one thing is indisputable: *When the gift comes from God, it not only makes you free and happy, it also makes those to whom you minister through that gift, happy because of the anointing.* Each of us has received grace-gifts from God. And, "as each has received a gift," we are to use it to serve one another, as good stewards of God's varied grace. We are given these gifts for the "progress and joy" of one another's faith.

Growing up. In all my years of growing up in the Virgin Islands and the many days spent kicking it on the Island with my best buds, it never once occurred to me that because I belonged to God, I had been given a gift or that my gift might be different. Neither had it occurred to me that I was different. Of course, everybody's unique, but this is what I mean. The "in between" ages (9-12 years old) have always been a tricky time for kids. For example, according to the Center for Disease Control, the average weight for a 12-year-old boy is 90 pounds. At this age, boys in the top 10 percent weigh about 120 pounds or more while those in the lower 10 percent weigh about 70 pounds or less. Now a lot of guys where I lived came in at around that weight, but I didn't even weigh in at the 70 pounds. They also say that television was a huge pull for this "in between" age group because boys do not usually know what else to do with themselves. A lot of kids my age were into the sitcoms and sat in front of the television every chance they got. Well, I wasn't into a lot of television back then. For one thing, we only had one set. It was black and white, and if I recall correctly, it was only 13 inches. We had to crowd around to see it and since I was pretty small, I did not worry about it very much. I don't think this had anything to do with me. I believe this had everything to do with God's design and plan for His children.

Contrary to the popular belief that one's sunset years are the hardest; my own judgment and life experience suggests that the period designated as "youth" is possibly the most challenging. It is a frustrating time in life because it is that period when one is hardly old enough to be on his own, and yet one has a strong sense or awareness of self.

The Lord recognizes the value of youth to His divine cause and chooses us when we are at a young age. No matter how we look at it, young people can be quite impetuous and sometimes a bit silly as they attempt to take their place in the world, but they also have a lot of energy and are a wonderful resource in the kingdom of heaven. Their hearts are filled with dreams and visions of the future with all sorts of possibilities. Even with fear striking at their hearts, they are still daring and adventurous. They will "go." Young people can accomplish magnificent things for the Master's cause. Man does not always recognize this but the enemy knows it full well and uses every opportunity to strike while in our youth.

I was rather lean and lanky back then, in more ways than one but looking back over my life, it is clear that God gave me the ability to stand. He strengthened me physically, mentally, emotionally and spiritually, in order that I would be able to "go" in the power of the Lord's might. He wants us to rely on Him and go in the power of His might. I did not realize this all those years ago.

All those years ago, I regularly dreamed and made plans about what I was going to do "one day" to make my mother and father proud of me. I was determined that one day I would fill in that blank space on my epitaph so that it says more than "He was born, and he died." I can remember little snatches here and there, right on through the sixth grade, where I was thinking about "one day." While other kids were hanging out, I was thinking on these substantive kinds of things and talking to God.

Years ago I would close my eyes real tight and imagine what things would be like "one day." If I concentrated real hard, I could see images that do not really resemble much of anything. If I strained against the darkness and rolled my eyeballs around a little, I could almost create any geometrical image I wanted. I have always done this since I was a child and it never occurred to me that this might not be ordinary until one day I mentioned it to someone who had absolutely no idea what I was talking about and looked at me real funny like I was crazy. Nonetheless, I had discovered back then that when I fell into a relaxed state (not sleeping and fully aware of my surroundings), I could sometimes see images: faces and people, but mostly things. They were all very fluid and in a constant state of change.

Now that I have grown up, I still wonder about that phenomenon and why some people have ability to do that while others do not. It was just one of those things, I suppose. But on the other hand, you see, I was dreaming. Without any relation to the natural "external" world or even my inner world, could this "closed eye" visual experience have anything to do with my love of music? If I concentrate real hard, even today, I can find myself recovering "still images" of my childhood or surroundings in which I became a person of profound thought. Perhaps somewhere in the recesses of my mind, was a desire to be an instrument of sorts, or perhaps a mouthpiece. People say I talk a lot and that I have the gift of gab. This is not necessarily connected to my interest in the saxophone but I wonder if that is supernatural. I have some sense that out of those early days of "one day" dreaming or fellowshipping with the Lord, came a great imagination and desire for a good future with God because it was during this period that I began to romanticize about playing the saxophone. God's gifts are without repentance.

As far back as I can remember, my whole world has revolved around Church. I am grateful because this is how I came to know and grow closer to the Lord. It has spiritually strengthened me, kept me grounded and has helped me to hold to worthy morals and standards. Many years of my life have been devoted to the Church of God of Prophecy, which was founded in 1903 on the isolated mountains of eastern Tennessee and western North Carolina. It soon became the second largest American Pentecostal denomination in America but did not receive a lot of public attention because its theocratic organization and ministry was tightly governed. It successfully avoided the limelight for more than two decades because, unlike other groups, its evangelists were not postured or broadcast as another popular voice in the nation. Despite that, the Church has undergone several transitions and even today, is still in transformation, there have been and continues to be many good days.

Bishop Stephens. Bishop Moses Stephens, founding father of the Church of God of Prophecy in the US Virgin Islands served as Overseer for more than 26 years. It was in 1946 at the Fish's Wharf that after much face time before God, prayer and fasting, that the Church was born. Bishop Stephens was considered the backbone of the Church. Things didn't feel quite right unless he was around. In fact, people referred to the US Virgin Islands Church of God of Prophecy as "Moses' church."

Although I was young, I felt the influence of this bond and was hooked into this connection in many ways. I remember hearing Bishop Stephens speak during many conventions. He was one of the great preachers of my young life and it was often said about him that we had "never heard such preaching." He had a strong, powerful voice and brought to many of his listeners more of a sense of God being present than other preachers. Other men were so intent on enticing the crowd that sometimes they came across like street vendors trying to pitch their wares. They completely forgot the true gospel message preaching sermons that were filled with clichés are often forgotten before you left the building. Even today there is such a strong desire to be clever and funny. However, with Bishop Stephens, it was different. He was not there to tickle our ears. When you left the service, you carried his message inside you for some time with a Spirit filled passion and determination to go on with the Lord. He was serious. We felt humbled by the Word. Our God was great and exalted. This preaching rightfully positioned me a child of God who should trust in the Lord. This was a gift.

One thing about Bishop Stephens, though, with that seriousness, was the length of time that we were in service. We were there every Sunday from 9:00am to 3:00pm. We would be so hungry until the corner of our mouths would turn white. Some of us were starving. I was about ready to kill something (or someone) so I could eat! But later when we were finally eating, it was with a blessed peace and thankfulness to God – not just for the food – but for the covering and intimacy that comes with being a part of the Body of Christ. The anointing would flow over that meal, and we would be grateful. I was gaining a quiet intimacy with God and my Church family. This was a gift. And yet no one spoke of it.

With this love of our souls, there was always something going on to make us think. I loved how Bishop Stephens would keep us in check – especially the young people. If you were singing a regular song or hymn, like *Amazing Grace*, for example, and sang it a little more progressively, it would sound very nice with every note in place. The crowd would enjoy it, often clapping their hands, standing or patting their feet enthusiastically. But after you were done singing, Bishop Stephens, being from the old school, would rise slowly and stand deliberately to his feet. Sometimes, we wondered if he did it for sheer effect. Then he would come out front and say, "You sang the song. Now we are going to sing the song like it should be sung – the right way."

All eyes would fasten on him. Then he would slowly take the song back to the old school way. Now the entire church was standing. He had a way with the crowd. Tears would be streaming down their faces. You would have thought God Himself had come down off the throne to see about the Gamble Gade church! Now, if you were the person that sang or played the song, you would get to see another level of the anointing as it flowed and ministered in that old school version of the song. Bishop Stephen's version was intended to be more inclusive of all the people, to remember where we came from and to make sure we would never forget our God. With Him, it was always about God. Though subliminal, this teaching was etched into my spirit as a child. This was a gift.

We all have fond memories of how precise Bishop Moses was and often marveled at his precision. He was the embodiment of perfection and correctness. Even if you could quote a passage correctly, he did not believe you truly knew that particular Scripture, unless you were able to cite the passage so we made a point to learn the Scripture references. If you quoted the passage, it must be exact or it was not correct in his eyes.

On certain occasions, the children had to go up to him and give the Scripture. We had to quote it correctly with the passage reference before returning to our seat. Once, when it was my turn, I went up to give John 3:16. I decided to confirm with him that it was the right passage before quoting. So I began with, "For God so the world, right?" I waited for his confirmation. "No," he boomed. I was startled and thought it over for a minute. I rolled the words to the verse around in my head, "For God so loved the world, that He gave His only begotten Son, that whosoever believeth in Him should not perish, but have everlasting life." I knew that was correct, so what was wrong? Then it clicked. Ah! I thought, he did not like the word "right"! So then I quoted the verse in its entirety, gave the biblical reference and waited. "Amen!" Bishop Stephens smiled. I returned to my seat, feeling proud. Man, that was close. I was sweating. I did not want to be embarrassed.

Thinking back on it, I realize this was precious because he was teaching us to study and realize that whatever we do, we must do it with excellence. We were taught to practice and realize that even if we got it wrong, we would have to accept the criticism, learn the lesson, and allow that humility to drive us to spend time with God and to rehearse until we got it right. This life lesson went into making me a child of God. This was a gift.

Life was exciting back then under Bishop Stephens. Though a man of authority, he was also a humble man who loved God and loved God's people. Out of the pulpit, Bishop Stephens was quiet and unassuming. His infectious smile and warm personality always struck me as a man of kindness. His willingness to extend a helping hand endeared him to countless church members and family at home and around the US Virgin

Islands. He gave his all to the ministry and faithfully served God and the people – for 26 years! Was this not a gift?

Over the years, I learned a lot and looked up to Bishop Stephens. My mother had a great respect for him and the Church. In fact, my mother did everything possible to support Bishop Stephens.

We were family. I mean like family for real. Frankly, I was a bit scared if he looked at me "just right" or in a certain way. He was the Church Bishop and could be rather foreboding. I remember the time he caught me hanging around outside of the church talking to some girl. I was just a kid and was half nervous anyway. It didn't take much to put the "fear of God" in me. Bishop got hold of me for good minute but he wasn't mean and gruff like some of the other men in the church. Still he caught me just right that day. Oh, this man had a way with the words – and so did my father! Yes, even this was a gift!

Joining the Church. Before Dad joined the Church of God of Prophecy, he was a part of the local Apostolic Faith ministry so he took me with him to church while my mom, my brother Ulric, and two sisters, Naomi and Ruth, went to the Church of God of Prophecy. One particular weekend, my mom told me they were going to have a Singspiration which was like a talent show. It was opportunity for everyone to showcase their talent. When I went there and saw the accoutrements and paraphernalia of the music platform as well as all the regalia for the other components of the talent showcasing, I was fascinated. There was real music with the Church of God of Prophecy Steel Band orchestra and all types of instruments. People came out with whatever talent they had. Some folks modeled different types of dresses and garments. Some ladies offered an exciting mix of local foods displaying their sweet moist coconut, pineapple, mango and guava tarts (Virgin Islands Style) atop their heads as they marched along with a beautiful assortment of other Caribbean delicacies. I remember it like it was yesterday. People who shared their creativity in an array of delicious refreshing beverages with tonics, maubi, sorrel and passion fruit juices were always winners and there were all sorts of colorful arts and crafts. I don't want to get too distracted but it was like having a food fair. Everyone was happy and lively and oh, the music was spectacular!

There was one group called the Prophecy Brothers. They had a great sound. When I heard them, I knew "that was it for me". I told Dad, "I'm done!" In my mind, I no longer wanted to attend the other church. In the Apostolic Faith church, my head would nod out all the time. It would bob up and down practically the entire service. They had one guitar, no drums, no piano or keyboards, no band. No offense to anybody, but there was nothing exciting there for me. Once I discovered all of that life in the Church of God of Prophecy, something came to life within me. Some of it registered with my "one day" idealistic dreaming. I was really stirred and though I was still only a kid, I knew enough to realize that it was time to leave. To me, I was being drawn from that place. This was a gift.

I left the Apostolic Faith and starting going with my mom to the Church of God of Prophecy. Then Dad came. My brother, Ulric, had joined the Job Corps, or he would have been there with us. Once Dad joined the Church, he was there practically every time the Church doors opened. The Church of God of Prophecy was the place to be in the Caribbean. If you were COGOP, you had it going on what with the singing, testifying and powerful preaching! The Church was rocking, not only with the music, but there was always a high time because of the awesome presence of the Lord. My father, who was bigger than life to me, was always present and accounted for and I was glad. All of this is part of who I am today.

As much as I loved the Church, a number of things happened somewhere along the way that awakened me from my childhood slumber. Until that time, I went about without much thought concerning the deeper issues of life.

Change in Leadership. In September 1970, the Church Of God Of Prophecy whose national headquarters is in Cleveland, Tennessee, officially appointed a bishop by the name of Harrison E. Price to serve as the Territorial Overseer of the British and US Virgin Islands. That was an eye opener for many of us. You see, in the US Virgin Islands, we are mainly of Danish and British descent and of course, some of the natives were of European and African extraction. The islands are replete with history and some incredible people from all walks of life, of different creeds and colors. They are a melting pot of diversity and culture. Today, the Virgin Islands population is 78% black, 10% white and 12% other with 81% of the population being of West Indian background and only 49% native born. While the population may seem largely the same and residents may outwardly express nationalistic pride as Americans and Virgin Islanders, they do not forget their heritage. Though it is an ensemble of different groups, the Virgin Islands are largely Black West Indian. To put a Caucasian in this position over the people would be an interesting change.

Now the Church taught that, after conversion, a believer should seek the blessing of sanctification as the "second work of grace." This cleansing experience placed an individual in a position to seek a third work in the spiritual progression: the baptism of the Holy Ghost, which was accompanied by speaking in tongues. This was the primary trademark of all Pentecostals many years ago. If you were filled with the Holy Ghost, you had a certain demeanor that kept you in agreement with the decisions that came down from Headquarters, General Assembly. With this in mind, we seemed to be getting along just fine. We were totally submissive.

Bishop Price. Regardless of our submissiveness, we were quite surprised when it was announced at the General Assembly who would be the new Territorial Overseer, but even more so when Bishop Price showed up at the local church at No. 20 Gamble Gade, and for several other reasons. He did not have history with the natives or local members; nor did it appear that he wanted to connect with us. Now I was in those formative years and at the age where I was desperately trying to become a man like my father and personally had never really thought about matters of racism. Like many people, our beliefs about life are based upon assumptions and our judgments about people are based on little evidence. I simply made the assumption that every General Assembly appointed leader in the Church, being saved, was perfect, loved everybody else in the Church and that everything would "be alright." It never occurred to me that within the Church, there were different levels of racism and perhaps even somewhat of caste system. This was quite disturbing because this was something that is inherently impossible to reconcile in our spirit man. Yet as Paul says in Philippians 4:12-13 we also "know how to be abased, and how to abound."

There were other questionable things about the Church that made it interesting but they were embraced because we had biblical points of references. For example, members were expected to abstain from alcohol, tobacco, secret societies and labor unions. As a kid, I wasn't so much bothered about those things, but I sure did have some thoughts about the carnivals, the movies, chewing gum, soft drinks and other things that were considered sinful. For the most part, even though somewhat challenging to people's minds, these were never deal breakers. In those days, the majority of the church members loved and desired to please the Lord. No one complained too much. Of course, there was always the legalistic group that was fixated on what you could and could not do, but the way I saw it, these things would neither make nor break me. There were a few things that I questioned quietly of myself. Though I never said anything to anybody, I never quite understood how we Island folks, living right in the middle of the Atlantic Ocean and the Caribbean Sea, could sit in silence and agree to some things. Like, not go swimming with the opposite sex? This was craziness to a lot of folk. I was very glad that I wasn't a female. I cannot say how many times I watched some of the girls strolling on the beach as hot as it was, remained in full dress. This was like being thirsty, walking right up to the water but not taking a drink. What a sacrifice.

But everything was locked down back then. No makeup or sleeveless outfits for the women. No muscle shirts for the guys. Men and women sat on opposite sides of the church. If you wore jewelry, it was the high point of church gossip. When we described someone, we might refer to them as, "the lady with the earbobs" or "the man with a gold chain around his neck" or perhaps the "girl wearing the short dress." Of course, the dress was probably only two inches above the knee. There were other things, too, back them. Maybe I did not care so much about the jewelry or dancing, but I did like sports. I truly believe we are going to be surprised when we see who makes it to glory!

While no one can deny that the Church of God of Prophecy had its share of problems, we know that Jesus never gave us the option of giving up on His Church. He certainly would not approve of us "hating" her. Therefore, it is impossible to follow Him while shunning the Church that He died to save. It is true that the Church has gone through some significant changes over the years. There were some errors, wrong teachings, misunderstandings and mistreatments. However, the reality is that we are human and regardless of what happens within the Church, God is using it around the world to transform lives and accomplish His will on earth. In many ways and in many places it is healthy and focused on fulfilling God's mission. This is a gift!

Chapter 2
Understanding your Worth and Value

"Music can change the world because it can change people."

Bono

There is no higher calling for you than to be who God called you to be. For those in the music ministry, this involves a lot of responsibility, a strong sense of vocation or call, and faithfulness. A church musician who has a strong sense of purpose in making music for the church and who is willing to live out the call on their lives in the experience of God's grace, will be able to thrive wherever they serve. One must be willing to grow in musical experience and still remain faithful to their unique gifts, but it is also important to keep the focus on the call. Every musical experience will not be at the top and as Temi Peters put it, "God is not looking for incredibly high notes, intricate riffs or award winning ad-libbing. God is looking at the heart." Our desire should be to allow ourselves to be His instrument.

We must guard against thinking more highly of ourselves than we should and at the same time, we must guard against sinful discontentment. Even so, if you do not understand your worth and value you will be functioning in an abnormal position. As a result of this situation you will find yourself constantly being cut short by life's situations and circumstances. We often feel that we are not as gifted as we would like to be, or that our gifts don't receive enough recognition, or that we would prefer another set of gifts altogether. First and foremost, God gives us gifts and talents for His glory. Then He places us strategically where we should be. As we honor and obey Him, our gifts bless others as they sanctify us. This is exactly what we need. None of God's plan is by accident. This is also one of the reasons it was important for me to understand my Church history. Many people have lived their Church's history without understanding the impact upon their lives. During Church of God schism, many wonderful people left the Church altogether rather than choosing one of the optional divides but I could not walk away. Instead, I embraced my upbringing in the Church and began to connect the tangible dots of my life. Although I have some connection to the past, I needed to study this history in order to make sense of where we are today and in context of understanding my value and worth. There were so many different personalities, events, cultural divides, timelines and circumstances that shaped today's church. There is no harm in exploring these matters because the truth is liberating.

As a result of researching a few books and articles from a broad spectrum of sources, it is evident that there were many factors which shaped the church over the years. It is easier to see more clearly how the Spirit of God worked in the lives of imperfect, but highly dedicated people to shape a faith movement that continues to play a vital role in God's unfolding purposes today. As a result, I have gained even greater confidence that the same Spirit that saw the church through seemingly insurmountable challenges in the past will continue to sustain and guide us in the future. Sometimes we go through struggles and endure pain but somehow, by the Holy Spirit, we manage to make it to the other side.

Church of God of Prophecy. The Church of God of Prophecy sprang forth out of the Church of God of Cleveland, Tennessee during a split in the 1920s. When A.J. Tomlinson, then the head of the Church of God (Cleveland, Tennessee) was ousted, he and his followers established what is now the Church of God of Prophecy. The Church was divided on such issues as civil rights. Many members, similar to many white southerners, exhibited a deep-seated racial prejudice toward blacks. Like most southerners, these church members viewed and accepted discrimination and segregation as a way of life, arguing that blacks were descendants of Ham and therefore cursed so they should be content with a lowly place in society. Their condescending attitudes were skillfully disguised as paternalistic views in an attempt to make the black man feel satisfied in his downtrodden condition and to coerce him into persuading others. There were all sorts of emotions because of the aftermath of the Civil War and Reconstruction. Support for segregation from middle-class black leaders reinforced paternalism among southern whites and convinced them that most blacks were satisfied with the status quo. During the struggle for rights in the South, black Church of God members too, while avoiding violence, fought for equal rights in the white male-dominated church.

Although the Church of God began as an interracial religious sect, there was constant strain against it. During the struggle, everything was done to keep the black church under control of white leadership. Many black clergymen and laymen felt isolated, subjugated to an all-white leadership, and in some ways, almost betrayed by the white brethren. Either way, the paternalistic bias that was so pervasive in the early Church of God slowly began to fade in the 1950s due to multiple complex factors. It is simple enough to say that sufficient pressure and confrontation was applied in the right places with help from white progressive supporters who wanted the church to integrate. By the mid-1960s, significant progress was made to force major changes in society.

When we talk about struggles, we usually think only about our pain. We often miss the fact that workouts and challenges help to prune and clear out the weeds. Offenses can propel us forward – but woe unto the one who causes the offense!

The Church slowly made important changes as it embraced the growing sophistication of younger, better-educated members who followed middle-class values but still showed signs of overt attempts to keep some black congregations under the control of paternalistic whites. Now, most followers of Christ understand that when Jesus ascended to the Father, He left one group in His place to carry on His mission: the Church. If we don't take the necessary steps to do everything possible to understand who we are and our role as the Church, then we are not taking Jesus' mission seriously. By God's own choice, the continuation of His plan of redemption now rests on the church.

In the Church of God of Prophecy, there seemed to be a lot of love, most of it bridged by the wonderful music, but still with underlying challenges. We also seemed bound to the Pentecostal way and a set of principles that offered escape from suffering and hope for a better life, if not in this world then surely thereafter. The doctrine was radically fundamentalist and everything about it was austere with its puritanical code of personal morality. We could not do anything "fun" – not that most of us wanted to – but also we were not the only church group. Almost everything back then was considered "worldly." We did not dare to even speak of thinking about such things as going to carnivals, movies, swimming or to a game of sorts.

For decades, the Church of God of Prophecy was indisputably the most racially inclusive Pentecostal denomination in the United States. There was some race mixing of appointments at local, district, state and national levels. Those many years ago, should it have mattered whether the overseer was black or white? Even though I was in the US Virgin Islands and not truly aware of the extensive racial concerns going on in the southern states, there was a trickle down affect of what was happening in Headquarters.

Growing Pains in the US Virgin Islands. It was during the early stages of this is when Bishop Price came to the Islands. It was then that we experienced, for the very first time as a ministry, some level of disenfranchisement. It was already questionable that the appointed leader would be white, but the 'elephant in the room' was huge.

Have you ever used a machete? The machete is powerful for clearing brush. In the tropics, machetes are ubiquitous, all-purpose tools. They are used to carve trails through tropical forests, slash out clearings for crops, crack open coconuts and slice papayas. They can keep weeds out of your garden, and, of course, they can be very imposing as weapons. A machete is razor-sharp and has no emotions. It just does what it was designed to do. There are tools that are used to sharpen us, pave the way, crack open places, heighten our awareness, shave some stuff off, train and make us into what God wants. Whether small or large, machetes have a way of shaving off some things that must be severed once and for all. God has a way of cleaning us up, maturing and preparing us.

Losing Bishop Stephens. Why would Bishop Stephens be required to go to the remote Leeward Islands after having founded, built up and worked so hard in serving over the Virgin Islands for 26 years? Should he have to begin a new work from ground up at this time in his life? Was there a precedence for this among white congregations? Was this something that the people should be questioning? Are we not sheep?

On the other hand, the new overseer did not have any track record with the Islanders and to our knowledge, no record of having done the field work required to build up this faithful following of people. To many, it was a stinging slap in the face to all of the work that had been done. There was concern regarding what was to become of Bishop Stephens. Would he have the inspiration and strength to repeat those 26 years in a remote village? Were the financials a factor in the decision? What viable reason was there for not sending the incoming Overseer to oversee work on this remote island instead? Didn't he have more strength? Wouldn't he be able to garner more support from General Headquarters than Bishop Stephens? Was the newcomer salaried also by General Headquarters? There were many questions and some unrest. Well, grumbling and complaining was never received well by the Lord, so the people were careful. However, they did speak up regarding concern for Bishop Stephen's welfare.

The children of Israel spent 40 years in the wilderness as a result of murmuring against Moses. We had our Moses. Was this new Overseer a Moses? Had he come to deliver the children out of bondage? Had God sent Him there? Once Moses died, who did God appoint? Joshua the son of Nun, was from the tribe of Ephraim. He had been with Moses. He was part of their history. Joshua was one of the greatest generals in human history. He had great faith, prevailing because God gave him the victory and he had zeal for bringing his own people on into the Promised Land.

He was connected with Moses.

The Israelites were God's people and he interacted with Moses and subsequently Joshua concerning the deliverance of these people. Some would make it to the Promised and some would not. There was a time of pruning and preparation. Not everyone made it into the Promised Land. God even said Moses would not be able to go. However, God promised to be their God and they were to be His people (*Jeremiah 30:22*).

There were some individuals who walked in this covenant knowledge and they believed God. But others began to speak against the Church and God's plan for their lives. Nothing on the earth is perfect, but when we speak against what God has ordained, we are getting into dangerous territory. What are the alternatives to what God offers? The children in the wilderness made such great complaint about wanting quail and not wanting manna that God gave them enough quail until it came out through their noses and killed many of them with a great plague.

Even through the turmoil, new leadership, changes and separations, there were some men who refused to complain about the path upon which God had placed them. Perhaps it was a test before promotion or strengthening the bonds of unity. Who knows? Either way, it is important to be aware of God's presence in your life and to watch your tongue. It is better to pray for God's intervention rather than try to take matters in our own hands – even for matters in our everyday life. We are to pray for our enemies.

Church is perhaps one of the few social institutions where dignity, protocol, respect, and reverence are maintained. The people were very disappointed about the newly appointed overseer, but many set about trying to accept the decision and move forward with the change. Many said nothing; it was a matter for the Lord.

When we come to the church and its services we are entering the Kingdom of God on earth, His habitation, and we choose to honor this sacred place by our attentiveness to what is proper and ordered. We have the opportunity to reflect the image of Christ within us by our actions.

No. 20 Gamble Gade Takes a Stand. People stayed quiet for awhile. However, sometimes, it is important to rise up and take a stand. Bishop Price, unfamiliar with the customs, culture or the ways of the Island people, had inadvertently postured himself over the people in a way that came across as authoritative, domineering and condescending. He moved too quickly to gain control over the administration and business operations of the church and his somewhat abrasive leadership style alienated the people almost immediately. While we don't know the entire story, we do know the effects of the change.

Members were suddenly treated as if in some sort of class system. It came across as racism to many. In certain instances, what should have been solved by church etiquette, training, and through committees or administrative staff, Bishop Price took a dictatorial approach. For example, commanding from the pulpit that children could not go to the restroom was not received well. This was only one of many things that went wrong with this particular appointment.

Somehow, things escalated to the point that finally a small group of people contacted General Headquarters to report their concern. Quite naturally, Bishop Price was offended when he learned of this action and almost immediately, called a business session. What happened next will be seared in my mind and in the memories of every member for the rest of our lives.

The Gamble Gade No. 20 Church was a fully operational 400-member strong ministry at that time with every auxiliary functioning. The discontentment during this time was not only about this foreign style of leadership but was also due to the apparent dismissal and lack of respect or honor for the foundational work done by our previous Church leader under whom the members had served with joy for many years. Bishop Price called the business meeting and put the members out of the sanctuary into the vestibule area while he remained in the pulpit. He went down the membership list and called out the names of everyone and asked each one whether they had any part in or contributed to the planning of the letter and complaint. Anyone who answered "yes" was declared a goat and called back in from the entrance hall and ordered to sit on the left with the goats; others who did not take responsibility for any part in the letter were declared a "sheep" and were instructed to be seated on the right with the other sheep. This deliberate and public confrontation was intended to humiliate and alienate those who had been bold enough to raise the concerns to Headquarters about the Church leadership in the US Virgin Islands.

Unfortunately, Bishop Stephens, who went on to the Leeward Islands as appointed, seemed to change later in life. In some ways it was disappointing to hear that his talk changed but he was being transparent in all that he said. He said that he had preached certain things that were not true; and that he did not believe those things anymore. I think there may have been a lot of confusion after the teachings in the church changed. Who knows how these things will affect a man? Our trust must always remain in the Lord.

It was rumored that Bishop Stephens went blind later in life. However, the light went out of the eyes of many people from that day. There was something about this particular period of time that raised not only my personal awareness of injustices in the United States from an emotional standpoint, but because I had never run into this kind of situation, it also raised my spirit man's consciousness. I found myself drifting into that "one day" place more often and later in the night.

Life has a strange way of affecting the cerebellum, or midbrain, where our deep emotional responses lie. I yearned to express myself through music – it's not like I could put into words all that I was thinking. That's the big mystery of music: you're just making the air vibrate, but you're definitely communicating a lot about how you feel about life. Around this time, it was easy to be in touch with a feeling of another time or something.

Perhaps this new Bishop was only following guidelines himself; maybe he wanted to take matters into his own hands and resolve the matter without outside assistance. I never knew about that and never really cared whether he treated Europeans differently than non-Europeans. My concern was that the Islanders should not be treated with disrespect nor taken for granted.

Personal growing pains. Seeing how our people were treated by the newcomer was very disturbing and raised a red flag concerning what my adult life would be like. I was mistreated at some very low points of my young life when compassion should have ruled and reigned in the lives of men of God. I was just a young boy, but when men seated in powerful places, had unkind, discouraging words for the least among them, I felt helpless. I told God about it. Sure, I got angry sometimes, but instead of harboring resentment, God suffered me to take my pain and rejection to Him at the foot of the cross. It was there that humility set in and I gave over my cares to God.

Despite hot tears of anger and frustration, out of me arose a desire for God to teach men the love of Jesus Christ. I prayed that He would keep me pure in heart, that I would always be able to hear Him. It was important to have a heart for God and His people. Whatever God's heart desired would also be mine. I would never want any harm to come to someone who had mistreated me. I wanted to be like Jesus and show the love of Christ. This was integral to understanding my worth and value.

On the job, there have been occasions where someone attempted to sabotage me or my work ethic. Even though I had the power to disarm, terminate and annihilate them, God spared me from taking advantage of my position to commit that action. Instead, I prayed for them for I saw them through different eyes. They were like sinful, disobedient children who needed a lesson but I knew if I did not pray for them, it was very possible that God would destroy their future for seeking to do harm against His child. I belonged to Him and I knew He could choose to avenge me. It was tough but the Lord was teaching me to be like Him. I was beginning to understand my worth and value.

One day, we want those who would otherwise go to hell, to come to Christ instead and be forgiven of their sins so they can also know the joy that we have in Him. Similarly, when leadership is out of order, we have to pray that they will be willing to accept correction. Our desire is that all men come into the fellowship of Christ.

Understanding our Worth and Value in the Church. Our gifts are not an accident of genetics and experience. God knew what he was doing when he made each of us and intentionally gave us the gifts in the measure we should have. Our gifts are not intended to be platforms where we try to gain our sense of significance from the esteem of men. Our real significance comes from God choosing us in Christ, gifting us, and deploying us in his kingdom for his purposes. There is more significance there than we can fully comprehend and appreciate. The praise of men is usually vicarious fluff. In other words, we are on assignment from God. This is why Paul says, “Only let each person lead the life that the Lord has assigned to him, and to which God has called him” *(1 Corinthians 7:17)*. “You are not your own” *(1 Corinthians 6:19)*. You are “a bondservant of Christ” *(1 Corinthians 7:22)* and a steward of the gifts you have received. Others need the benefit of your gifts in operation. That’s why you have them.

Our lives are not about pursuing our individual dreams. Many of our dreams are self-exalting pride fantasies and gratuitously selfish when we really examine them. And the truth is, we rarely know what’s best for us and what will really make us happy. But our Designer knows. He knows exactly what were made for and how we can live to the fullest and be most fruitful. He will lead us in the most ultimately fulfilling paths. We should live our assignment and steward our gifts to the utmost for God’s glory and for the sake of others.

We should not dishonor God by devaluing the gifts He’s given. Sometimes it will require taking a stand whether it means suffering criticism, sacrificing your comfort level, or risking your reputation.

Grumbling about gifts you don’t have or resenting others for the gifts they do have is a waste of valuable time. In instances where others are prideful in displaying their gifts, we need to pray for them. “So, brothers, in whatever condition each was called, there let him remain with God” *(1 Corinthians 7:24)*. There is no higher calling for you than to be you, and

God will reward you beyond your wildest dreams if you faithfully steward your gifts.

Once your worth and value is established between God and you, you must begin to function in that calling and gift without being fearful or having worries about executing it. Once your worth and value is diminished it will be difficult to bring it back into fruition. In order to feel good about yourself, you must see yourself as a person of worth and value.

People often take their gifts and talents for granted, underestimating their value and failing to recognize the significance. You must take precaution against anything that undermines your credibility, musicianship or authority of your ministry. We live in a time when everybody and their sister can and does make their own music. It doesn't mean, however, that they can produce music fit for the house of God. Musicians who want to be taken seriously should endeavor to gain proper respect and take responsibility for setting the tone for discussions concerning your music.

Being a musician takes a lot of creative, energy whether it involves constructing masterful musical arrangements or simply following a flat routine. Even if you have a natural talent for a certain instrument, there's a difference between "playing an instrument" and "being a musician." That difference involves practice. Musicians are dedicated to improving their skills and learning new techniques and more complicated music on the instrument they've chosen. The only way to do that is with regular and serious practice which ultimately translates into time. Benjamin Franklin said "Time is money." We should be good stewards over both. Therefore, taking your talents and gift lightly undermines all of the time and effort involved in perfecting and producing a quality service to the people. It is impossible to instill public confidence and respect for you if you lack confidence in yourself.

People will take your talents and gifts for granted if you allow it by over indulgence. Art valuation generally involves estimating the potential market value generally based on supply and demand, aesthetics and subjective cultural views. Apart from that, it is simply a reflection of what the highest bidder is willing to pay. Most artists have to be schooled on how to create a pricing structure which involves their time and materials with mark ups, comparables, trends in the economy, and uniqueness. The ruin is brought on or hastening by flooding the market with a lot of copies. The gift's value increases by its impact to please or satisfy. We devalue and hasten its ruin by over indulgence which sets oneself up to cheapen the costs associated with the execution. Talents and gifts are not cheap. God gives excellent gifts of value which bring forth great merits of reward and end results. Therefore, the person must fight very hard to ensure their gifts and talents are not lost. Worth and value must resonate in a person's heart, soul and mind.

I did not understand my worth and value so I often did odd jobs for people, thinking I was making a difference in my life by extending good will toward them. Actually, I accomplished nothing in terms of functioning in my gift. For example, I may have worked hard to complete a job at a discount rate because I wanted to help them. However, since I was not functioning in my giftedness nor in talent, it was neither wholly complete nor rewarding in the sense of the satisfaction that comes with the intended use of God-given gifts and talents.

In retrospect, it is clear that as church musicians, we are somewhat uncomfortable when it comes to understanding our worth and realizing our potential. We do not feel comfortable at expressing salary or compensation requirements because we have been taught to believe it is either shameful or wrong to be paid for services. Many of us know how to command a salary in the secular world but because we fear criticism or labeling from the church we attend, we often allow the church unfounded liberty.

There have been many debates on whether church musicians should get paid – as many pros as there are cons. We should have a little Straight Talk in order to hash out some of those points.

During those times of my personal experiences, I could have utilized my talent in ways which potentially would have opened doors for me in that particular field. It is important to not misunderstand the importance of the gifts and then of the worth and value.

When I made sacrifices to do odd jobs or some work on the side to help people at a discounted rate, many of those same people would turn around and ask me to perform at some function they were sponsoring or supporting. In almost every case, it was without proper compensation. It did not reflect appreciation for my talent. It did not adequately cover the time involved or required to rehearse, provision, transport, equip, configure and perform the service. We should be willing to generously give of our time, talents, and means to the Church. However, not to the point of abuse. In some churches, the expectation has been set that you must give everything you have to the church and that you must be at the disposal of the church anytime you are needed. That is not Scripturally based and has often resulted in burnout and a decrease in attendance. Singular dependence upon an individual for a specialized, professional talent is different from a general calling, nontechnical gift and casual participation.

We must be equipped with wisdom. The whole intent of the good news is we have a Savior and a right to eternal life. With this Savior, we have access to healing, deliverance, and liberty. Church members who have professional backgrounds in medicine and law are quite talented. They could offer pro bono services in some ministerial capacity. Yet, how often does this happen in the church "for free"? How often are these talented, spiritually gifted people asked to bring these services, to counsel or minister to someone in the church? Can we not worship God through these gifts? The evangelist, prophets, and ministers all speak the Word, but it is rare that they serve in such capacity without the expectation of an offering. It is highly unusual for visiting ministers, especially those who are well known, with large followings, to come without some discussion concerning expenses.

People have often requested my services as a favor and do not feel they should pay me. Most of them think you simply show up with your instrument and start playing. Of course, you can always ask them whether a stipend or an offering is extended with the invitation but that leaves it in their court. It seems the church musicians struggle more than any other industry and this should not be. All professional musicians, whether secular or non-secular, should provide a business card listing an array of services, booking agent contact information, or how to get in touch with you concerning how to secure you for the event. Any unwillingness on their part to respect your requirements does not diminish your gift! Of course, God will take care of you if you decide to do a concert for free. However, if musicians prefer to give away their services, they should not complain when they are broke. It is not proper to complain after voluntarily making a sacrifice.

Church people have little or no understanding of what goes into the preparation and do not view music performance as a service. They will never know unless it is brought to their attention. Most church people have 1) been led by leadership to trivialize or diminish a musician's worth 2) not been properly educated on the value of music in the church 3) no understanding what goes into the bottom line costs 4) little or no respect for the ministry of the music or 5) felt licensed to have premium music rendered for free.

We have seen this reflected in today's world during the decline of modern music industry. It's almost a rite of passage that every artist goes through today. Artists now have to accept not being able to rely on music sales to sustain a career. Downloading music off the internet is what fans do today. They are buying differently than they once did. Music sales are being handled through other types of performance management. However, when an artist has to bear expenses, give time, and show up in person – and with a good attitude – the hosts and fans are expected to adequately compensate the person. If there was an invoice breakdown associated with each performance, we would see line separate lines of service and products detailing the leasing of equipment, peripherals, instrumentation, vocals, attire, flat rates, consultations, stage presence, accompaniment, travel…and the list could go on and on.

If a musician is not paid to play the music at the church, that musician will have to be paid to do some other job and that would mean not having the time required to give proper attention to the music job. The church music could become an afterthought. Churchs with the proper understanding will have the foresight to understand something else. This may explain why a lot of musicians have taken their talents, departed the church and have sought to earn a living in the secular arena. They can go to a club and either if it's meager beginning, they do get paid and appreciated.

Paying the musician(s) should be based upon how the music department impacts and is able to encourage attendance and support the ministry. Whether the church is a start-up or has been around for some respectable number of years, it is necessary to set the right precedent. If people learn from the beginning that they have to pay for the rendition of church music, it will not be a problem in the future.

If it becomes necessary to replace existing musicians, it would already be in the budget and therefore easier for the Church to allocate funds for the replacement.

As I sit here reminiscing for a moment, I can smell my mother's cooking – especially the peas and rice and goat meat, my favorite. The flavor was mild and not overpowering -- just enough to give it a hint of that island flavor. She also baked the most wonderful pastries and sometimes on Sundays, some of the church folk would stop by to pick up a coconut pastry. Other days, she would expect me to make deliveries for her. I loved those days. If I close my eyes real tight right now and lean my head way back, like so, I can still hear her voice calling me. "Ira, Ira!" she would call to me. "Off with you now, and hurry back." Without hesitation, I would hop onto my 10-speed yellow and black bicycle, first with a friendly pat for Dar-Rey, my German Shepherd, before heading down the road. I was quite happy to do this job. For all of the many deliveries over the years, one would think I would have gained more weight from the pastries that never made it to their destination! Once upon a time life was so sweet! Who would have thought it could get so complicated.

Can we talk for a minute? Sometimes, we need to "tell it like it is", as they would say. If I had a few words to say, first I would speak to the musicians.

To Musicians and Vocalists. Whatever you do, you must remember that the congregation is made up on individuals who have different sensitivities. They need to hear their own voices and they need to participate in the worship and praise service. If they cannot hear themselves, they may opt out or become disinterested and even annoyed if the music is so overpowering that it dulls their senses. If the organ is always playing, they can drop out without anyone noticing. So bring it – as they say – but bring it right. Turn down the noise so people can hear. Although we should keep the tempo moving, it does not always have to be tailored to the most upbeat tempo. We should be sensitive to the move of the Holy Spirit. Sometimes it is alright to be quiet. People in musician ministry – that includes the musicians - should attend services even when they are not on program. If we keep an eye on God in everything we do and aim at pleasing him more than ourselves, He would show up in our services. We need to learn to do a mix of music that reflects our audience and to help us grow and understand our community. One-sided music reflects a lazy music department. Tossing the old hymns out in favor of contemporary music that is only about praising God for something He has done and forgetting to worship Him just because He is, is a common mistake. Our congregations often get in the habit of feel good music, singing songs about how we feel when we love the Lord. Jesus said, "If you love me, feed my sheep."

Talking to the Church. I have one simple question: What is it about musicians that make the Church not want to pay them? Is it because they seem to enjoy what they do? That it seems effortless for them to render music and sing songs? The thing I often wonder is why those who disagree with paying musicians seem to be so angered about it? What about paying child care workers, the church secretary or the pastor? We don't seem to battle those – but we go up-at-arms if we have to pay someone to play a piano or strum a guitar. This is fascinating. This is also somewhat ignorant. There has been a lot of selfishness, inconsideration and taking our musicians for granted for years!

No wonder so many have left the Church. We have complained about them leaving but who is the Church? If we are the Church and we have mistreated people and not paid them as worthy of their hire, but we who sit in decision making positions have taken home a paycheck, then shame on us. I've heard all kinds of excuses but really, if we have the love of Jesus Christ in our hearts, we would do our best to love and honor people with His love. This reminds me of the silly bickering among the Pharisees and the Sadducees regarding the Sabbath. What foolishness was it that led people to believe that it was against God's law to administer healing on the Sabbath? God meets and communicates with us where we are.

If we would drive back through the historical pages of the Bible, we might discover that the interaction of God with man, was a reflection of human behavior. When God has conversation with us, it is in a language that we can understand. He uses words and terminology that man has adopted. When God promised Abraham he would be the father of nations all of which would be blessed because of him, was Abraham going to Sabbath every week? What do we know about him? Did Moses not kill a man? When Jesus met the woman at the well and spoke of the living waters, He knew she would understand the implications. How precious was water back then? How far and how often did one have to travel in order to have fresh cool water every day? What about times of famine? Do you think Jesus would have set up a rule to prevent the woman from having access to Him just because the law was that Samaritans didn't talk to Jews? And she was known for being with a number of men. What kinds of rules has the Church adopted to distress and even oppress the members?

When God told Abraham to sacrifice his only son, Abraham did not have to ask for an explanation. Man was already in the habit of offering up sacrifices.

For the sake of directness, I created *Straight Talk*, and deliberately placed it at the end of the book so that those individuals who have very strong feelings against compensating or providing a stipend to musicians may elect to ignore that section. My intent is not to offend, but to enlighten. Even Jesus reminded us that "Inasmuch as ye have done it unto one of the least of these my brethren, ye have done it unto me." (Matthew 25:40) While some people may not see the applicability of this Scripture, I wonder who made the decision that musicians do not deserve to be worthy of their hire? Will the real Church please stand up? Rather than belabor the point, more thoughts on this can be found in *Straight Talk and at the end of this book.*

Chapter 3
Staying Focused in Your Gift

The artist is nothing without the gift, but the gift is nothing without work.
Emile Zola

A person must understand why God gives talents and gifts to people. When God blesses you with a gift, the gift is meant to be for a life time. So He gives you a gift that you can use to glorify Him only. One thing the individual with the gift must understand is that the gift is not about you, but God. Staying focus simply means understanding what is required by God about you. Your mind has to be in order, and also your heart, body and soul must be in agreement. The individual must evaluate their mind with the intention of staying focused. Staying focused is a strong trait that God can use in a seasoned person with a sound mind. It is easy to give up -- that is a human reality. However, God changes that concept when you put your trust in Him.

Another Change in Leadership. The unfortunate circumstances that developed under the leadership of Bishop Price and the fallout that ensued consisted of enough damage to call for another change to come to the USVI. The next appointment from General Headquarters was not without some trepidation for the USVI, but generally speaking, it was a welcome change for us. The decision came in the middle of turmoil when people were a little wary and even disgusted to the point of leaving but this change would affect my personal future.

R.B. Finlayson. In September of 1971, the Church appointed a bishop by the name of R.B. Finlayson Jr., a headquarters representative who was sent to the United States Virgin Islands to serve as the Territorial Overseer of the Church of God of Prophecy in the U.S. and British Virgin Islands. This new overseer had no problem interacting with people of color and was a good fit for the local Church and for rest of the Virgin Islands.

As I think back on that time, I realize this was significant. After the previous year's series of disastrous events, the announcement of change in leadership was received with a resounding roar throughout the General Assembly populous. It seemed many people had felt the appointment of Bishop Price to the Virgin Islands was quite irregular and a bit unsettling. Even though most people had no idea about the circumstances that led up to the change, it was clear that they sensed something was not right about the previous year's decision appointment for Bishop Price.

The New Band. In March of 1974 the Lord laid on Bishop Finlayson's heart to organize a brass band. He presented this idea to the local Church Of God Of Prophecy located at No. 20 Gamble Gade in St. Thomas. Immediately after this idea was presented, many people of all ages were excited and eager to sign up to become a member of the Band. Prior to this time, I did not have any tangible interest in playing in a band. I mean, it is not like I had been sitting around practicing on an instrument hoping to be in a band, but I was definitely interested.

The idea of getting involved and engaged in positive, wholesome demanding Church activities was intriguing to me from a creative artistic standpoint but to my father, it was probably more from a parenting perspective.

Dad came to me and asked me what I thought. The word, "Trumpet" popped out of my mouth. I don't know why. I guess I was excited. But my dad said "I really like the saxophone. Why don't you try playing that instrument?"

I promptly signed up for the Band. I secretly thought that playing music was a cool thing to do. My dad and I had such a great relationship that I valued and honored his opinion. Not all kids are that way. I've heard of teenagers having horrible relationship with their fathers and they often do opposite of what their parents want out of resentment, anger or disobedience. Some parents are absent, abusive, alcoholic, unreliable or simply not unavailable. But my dad was the absolute best, always great at cheering me on to reach for my dreams.

Therefore when my dad asked me about trying to play the saxophone, something leaped inside and I got excited. His suggestion agreed with me. I saw how Bishop Finlayson's son (nicknamed Chucky) played the drums, and even toyed with the idea of learning how to play them. I had never heard drums played like that before by anyone. I felt like I could do anything with my dad supporting me. We talked about the different choices of instruments. I gave it a lot of thought before telling anyone my decision, but deep down inside, I already knew the saxophone was the instrument for me. It was distinct. People liked it. I would be able to express my inner self. Although I did not know it then, we would become as one instrument. It would be me – and the Sax. My dad would be pleased. Yes, I liked the thought of that.

From that day, I started envisioning myself playing in the band. Even before the band's first rehearsal and before I had even touched the saxophone, I could see myself standing on the platform overlooking the crowd with my eyes toward heaven. One day, I ran home and switched on the radio in the back room of the house. I heard the charging tempo and upbeat teasing tones of Andraé Crouch's *"The Choice."* This piece of music came on, and something just exploded inside. I'll never forget hearing Andraé for the first time. It was like someone had opened a whole new world of possibilities for me musically. The depth of his influence on Christian music is incalculable. I felt this rush of adrenaline and then emotions flooded through me. It was so intense. I fell on my bed so I could concentrate on the song and the notes. There was something in there that registered with me inwardly. It seemed less cluttered in that particular space. When the song was over, my mind raced with questions. I was thinking and wondering, wow, what just happened? A few minutes before I was somewhat discouraged and wondering if I would ever be able to play, but suddenly I was in a totally different place, no longer feeling alone. This was different from the regular music that I heard at church. Nobody really understands why listening to music — which, unlike food or other satisfying things that have no intrinsic value — can trigger such profoundly rewarding experiences. Somehow I knew this is what I wanted to do with the rest of my life. I needed to learn how to bring that level of enjoyment before the Lord and to His people.

Later, I found myself way up there somewhere, where the little bird of my grade school classroom was, soaring high above the clouds and looking down on these earthly matters that no longer seemed to matter. The instrument would blend with me. Now I was different and as I played, the world became different. I could see people around me through quite different eyes. I was happy during those times when, through closed eyes, I could escape and come back only for the essential things – perhaps long enough to eat and occupy the earth.

Staying Focused. I was 12 years old, when I began to play the alto saxophone. In some ways, life became a miserable experience. Oh, I guess I tried hard enough to be a good student but by most rules, I was probably only average. I was stressed a lot, though, about playing in the band. It was tough trying to come up to speed on my horn. I remember crying one day, saying: "I'm not ready, I'm not ready. When will I ever be good at this?" One time, I was upset for an entire week until the next time when we were supposed to play. I didn't tell anybody but I got headaches and stomach aches a lot.

Sometimes, I wanted to skip class; sometimes, I wanted to skip school. Other times I wanted to yell but at whom? Oddly enough, the one thing I never wanted was to get rid of the sax! I was always trying to find some place to practice my instrument. It was tough. There was no place to go. The horn was loud. I didn't get much sleep either. Sometimes I would slip downstairs after tossing around in bed trying to think through my notes and then would run outside down the street somewhere while everybody was sleeping. I had to find ways to try to make some runs on my sax.

I hated being the worst. After band practice, I couldn't let it go. I refused to quit. Someone once made a wisecrack and said maybe I should give it up, that maybe I had too much pride or maybe I was just plain stubborn. Well, maybe that could be true. I really like the feel of the saxophone in my hands and I liked the way I looked playing it. There was a lot more to it than that, however.

What a lot of people don't know is that when the saxophone first came out, many performers turned up their noses at it, because they preferred the lighter clarinet. It was new and just like anything else, it was unchartered territory. It is the only woodwind instrument that is not really made of wood. Many musicians resisted it for a long time because it looked like a clarinet but it was not a clarinet at all. It was different – like me. They laughed at it – like me, and flat out rejected it – like me.

It's creator gave the saxophone something extra. Unlike the clarinet, the saxophone had a beautiful curve and stage presence. It used a single reed and has an all-metal body, usually brass. Of all the band instruments, it was at the heart of controversy. The person who created it back in the 1840's was attacked and accused of making a "tool of the devil" for manipulating sexual desires with its sound. For years, the sax was associated with the military, Vaudeville and circus folks, African-American communities, and members of the lower classes, as well as general impropriety and questionable morals. Other bands and associations did everything possible to discredit it, calling it a misfit and anything to keep it from being accepted.

Now imagine this. My wanting to play this very instrument that was rejected, in the Church and to complicate things, I did not have the necessary skills to play it properly!

At the time, I didn't know much about saxophones but I knew my dad would do whatever it would take to help get me started. I learned everything I could about the sax.

The Martin saxophone has always been one of the most sought after collectible vintage brands around. Some of the product lines were fancy with names like "The Martin Sax", or Handcraft or Typewriter, and a variety made during 1919 to 1967. It was confusing, but what collectors now call the "The" Martin saxophones are ones that had "The Martin" engraved on the bell, with the type of sax, (alto, tenor, soprano, etc.) engraved above these words. Collectors rave about the quality of some of the old saxophones. From 1945 to around 1967, Martin made the line called "The" by collectors. They made student and intermediate saxophones in the 50's and 60's. The Martin is a popular collectible in the world of vintage saxes, and a brand that is held up as having a great sound as well as classy engraving and good looks. There were other manufacturers out there but guess which one my parents bought me? My first saxophone was a Martin saxophone that cost my parents about $150.00! Believe me, for my father to invest that kind of money in me at such a young age and without my having exhibited any skill to play it speaks volumes concerning my father's love for me and his faith in me. I determined within myself right then, that I would honor him with my dedication to learn how to play the Martin. And if I would honor my earthly father, how much more would I honor my heavenly Father!

I was getting used to the idea of playing the saxophone for my dad. When I thought of it, I savored it, picturing myself with the delicate instrument in my hands, the mouthpiece poised close to lips and ready. Once in a while, I would see my dad sitting right down front, giving me a nod of encouragement. "Play, son, play." I could almost hear him. Oddly enough, at other times, I had on sunglasses and the ladies were there. Where did that image come from, I would wonder. I always shoved that image way in the back of my mind. After all, I couldn't even play yet.

One afternoon, I startled myself with the different images I had in my mind about how I was going to look playing that horn. I couldn't help myself and started grinning a little bit. Then I started laughing and before long, my knees buckled. I was laughing so hard and was rolling back and forth on the floor. It was all just a dream. If I wanted to play that saxophone, I was going to have to stay focused. I heard my sister call out my name. "What's going on with Ira?" she called from down the hallway. "Is he carrying on again? What's wrong with him? I hear him all the way down here." Just then my brother walked around the corner and shook his head. "No problem. He is joking around again. I say he has lost it!" he answered and swatted me playfully. But I didn't tell anybody what I was thinking.

Onward Christian Soldiers. By this time, a lot of things had transpired. Bishop Price had come and gone. We had a new Overseer. But what happened with Bishop Price was no small matter. It seemed to start some sort of slow peeling away of the layers of mystery. Even though I was young, it was a pensive time in my personal life. I always had very strong beliefs. Outwardly, I went through the normal motions of a young man but something had changed deep within. I could not quite synthesize all of the mixed emotions and most certainly could not articulate how I felt. There was some anger, distress, uncertainty, disillusionment, and helpless.

It was as though the rug had been whisked out from under Gamble Gade. There was still an undercurrent within the Church as though something was not quite settled. It felt like two people in a heated disagreement who had come to an impasse but everything that needed to be said was still hanging in the thickness of the air. There was a lot of prayer going on but it was still unsettling.

What was this all about anyhow? What was the whole intent of the Church? How did things get all twisted up like this? How could we be united if we did not agree? What impact would this have on outsiders? What kind of impression would this make on the community? I began to examine my beliefs and the Church teachings against what I was seeing in light of what we had seen since Bishop Stephens was replaced. I did everything possible to put my finger on the pulse beat of truth. Were there different rules for different folks? Was there racism in the Church? How could we have come to this in the Church? I needed an outlet.

Everything in the natural took on a new look. Have you ever awakened from slumber with a little sleep in your eyes? As you rub them, things seem to get clearer. If put administer a few drops of Visine or your favorites eye drops in each eye, it will make images appear sharper. The ocean becomes clearer, the grass greener, the skies bluer and the horizon is endless. Now as I raced about on my bike delivering pastries and tossing newspapers for my cousin Kenneth, I found myself channeling all of those emotions into my rehearsals. When I patted our German Shepherd, Dar-Rey on the head and talked to him, it was from this new perspective.

Inwardly, something was driving and pushing me; something that wanted to burst forth at the seams. Even when I lazed around, there was something on the inside working me on the outside. There was no rest – even when it appeared I was calm and methodical, there was a part of me that wanted to cry aloud. For some reason, I held onto it as long as I could, keeping it all inside. Perhaps I was waiting for that "one day" that I knew would come. Besides, with all that Jesus went through, I guess I could endure this. Besides, He didn't die for me so that I would give up. I knew I must fight my way through the heaviness with praise.

Back then I did not understand what it took for my dad and mom to give me that saxophone but when I look back on it, I realize just how big a sacrifice it must have been. Even in the middle of all the challenges and obstacles that my mom and dad must have faced, they still managed to be interested in what I wanted. My dad wanted me to be the best that I could be and to give everything I had to whatever I did. That means a lot to me until this day. Perhaps this is the reason I put everything I have into playing the saxophone. My parents made me their priority and my dad was always there when I needed a listening ear. He was always concerned about my life and future. I could still hear him well after I had grown up, "Yes," he said in that deep baritone of his, "That's it, son, the saxophone. You are gifted. " I was determined that I would play.

The Face of Rejection. The Church flourished under Bishop Finlayson's leadership. He did a great job organizing the band. Still a shy kid trying to find my way in the music world, I was just learning to play and trying to get it together. The new brass band was organized with almost 60 members. The band was made up of trumpets, trombones, saxophones, clarinets, French horns, and drums. The saxophone section was comprised of three Tenor Saxophone players and nine Alto Saxophone players.

The new overseer made agreements that we would have Band practice every Saturday at the Charlotte Amalie High School in the Sugar Estate section in St. Thomas U.S. Virgin Islands. Although it gave me chills when I learned of this arrangement, I must admit to being somewhat nostalgic when it comes to that school. As the oldest public high school in the USVI, C.A.H.S. has produced some powerful men and women. When you leave that school, you have been provided the proper framework of knowledge and skills necessary to be responsible, productive citizens with ability to function in a global society. The music suite was added in 1964 and was real "sweet." Just a few short years after I moved away, Hurricane Hugo caused considerable damage in 1989, but C.A.H.S. is still very much a major backbone in St. Thomas. Most of St. Thomas' leaders in all areas of government, healthcare, education, business and commerce are proud alumni of C.A.H.S. You name it – they came out of that school: governors, attorney generals, educators, musicians, athletes, doctors, ambassadors, judges. They encourage students to strive for greatness and excellence. It is a noble school and I am proud of this part of my heritage.

However, it was also a tough school – probably tougher than most. There was no Mrs. Harrigan, my fourth grade teacher, to cheer me on and like a dear Mom, to stay on top of me and give me that extra push to make sure I got things done. The C.A.H.S. Band director, Mr. Charles Cox, volunteered his time and talent to the band by giving free music lessons to the Brass Band members. Mr. Cox was from Georgia, and was very articulate with his musical skills. We were beginners, but he was still stern and hard on us to get the music right and correct. I was in the ninth chair being the worst of all other alto saxophone players and though mortified to be placed in the very last seat in the section, I was determined I would work my way up in the section.

One of the players, Herbert Coakley, was extremely accomplished for him to be a beginner, and he knew how to read music notes very well. On the other hand, I was the worst player, and because of it, I got slammed a lot by the other band members. Chad Fowler said, “Always be the worst guy in every band you’re in - so you can learn.” I don’t know where on earth he got that idea! It was very difficult to learn with people teasing and mocking me because I could not play.

The Band instructor would stop the band right in the middle of the song we were practicing and ask me, “What type of cigarettes do you smoke?” He said this because my tone was so horrible. Admittedly, there is something about the saxophone that could set the listener on edge. Sometimes people think of saxophones as making a dreadful, dreary honking sound like a goose or like a throaty bark. The good players are able to make it produce a wonderful seductive creamy sound but even so the listener is always aware of the ‘noise’ element of the sound.

If the reed is too dry when breath passes down the airway, the agitation could produce a squeaking noise on top of the honking. The sound is not golden. The whole band would laugh and I wanted to go through the floor. This was a truly horrifying experience for a 12 year old kid who really wanted to do this well. It hurt my feelings but still I was determined. I kept coming to practice, bringing my horn and dragging my ego. The band really did not have any idea what they were doing. I didn’t know either; only God knew. Half the time I was frustrated; the other half I was furious. If I wasn’t one of those, I was fighting mad. I wanted to rise up out of that pit of hell and prove them wrong!

The band was being prepared to play for the Church of God of Prophecy United States and British Virgin Island Territorial Annual Convention that was held every year in the Virgin Islands. This would be our first major performance. While the members were encouraged by Bishop Finlayson’s exuberance and his dynamic messages, I was dealing with my own set of circumstances and facing a somewhat miserable time of life.

First of all, I was going through puberty. Secondly, I was struggling against a lot of jeering and rejection about playing the saxophone. Third, I had no place to safely practice my horn without criticism. This was before the days of the sound room. I would practice at home when I could but sometimes my mom would say to me when she’d had enough, “Ira could you please stop the noise with that saxophone!” It was terrible thinking my own mother could not bear the sound. Of course, if you have any idea or knowledge of how to play a woodwind instrument you know that at the beginning stages the sound and tone is unbearable. However, once you get past the "noise" and get successful on the horn, then everybody wants to hear you. There was no one better to cheer me on than my mom, for sure. She would be either on the front row waving her hands in the air or if on the back row, you could hear her all the way down front. She was always pumped up for me. Oh, yes, she let everybody know, "That's my son!" she would call out. I loved it. But until that time came, I had to find a way to rehearse. Most of the time, it was at the farthest point in the house. There is really nothing one can do but keep practicing. In my case, it got so bad until I had to take it to God. I needed somewhere to practice. Only God could fix this problem.

But after I made my prayer request and commitment to God, instantaneously my musical skills began to change, and I started to improve tremendously. God had honored my prayer and gave me the desire of my heart. Trusting in God, believing on him and his word brings lasting results. The scripture in *Psalms 4:2* reads: Hear me when I call O God of my righteousness, thou hast enlarged me when I was in distress; have mercy on me and hear my prayer. *Psalms 5:3* reads: My voice shall thou hear in the morning O Lord, in the morning will I direct my prayer unto thee, and I will look up. Finally *Psalms 36:5* reads: Commit thy way unto the Lord: trust also in him and he shall bring it to pass.

Still at band practice, they laughed when I showed up and pulled out my horn. It hurt. Sometimes, I could hear them before they could see me. But I kept showing up with a determined mind. Fourth, no one seemed sensitive to my plight – not even the Overseer. Bishop Finlayson attended No. 20 Gamble Gade. If I played and messed up, he would tell me publicly and without biting his tongue,"Son, don't play."

Rejection was very tough especially for early teens. If you embarrass a kid in front of a crowd, he's done. You can break his spirit at that age. And truthfully, I did not feel like playing anymore. But there is something about belonging to God. I kept going despite the odds and all of the horrible treatment. Somehow my eyes remain steadfast on the Lord. So I put all of that emotion and energy into learning and becoming whatever it was God wanted. I did not know exactly what it is I was striving toward. But I knew something was happening. I was being created and developed into a man of God but the wrinkles had not been ironed out yet and only the designer could see the pattern. What I was acutely aware of was that while other kids were hanging out on the stretch or spending time in the streets on the weekend, I was stealing away somewhere to a quiet place, trying to figure out who I was and how I was going to play that $150 saxophone.

Understanding the Dynamics. Anyone who ever lived in the Virgin Islands for any length of time knows there are no bad days on St. Thomas - well except for a hurricane and heavy rain once in awhile. Ok, so I never really had a bad day unless someone hurt my feelings and even then, I learned to get over it real quick. But generally speaking, there was not that much to do in St. Thomas for a kid who went to church all the time except for going to beautiful beaches. I didn't have much else going on with me. I mean I could hang out with the guys for awhile but for some reason, and I don't know when it happened, but a certain thought came to me and it lit up my whole head. I knew my world was going to be centered around playing the saxophone. Perhaps it was during the first time I heard Grover Washington. I nearly flipped.

One time my cousin, Angel Vanterpool, came to the house because his mom and my mom were going to sell pastries and Island tonics together. We borrowed my mom and dad's car. Well, actually, I might have taken it without permission. I don't think they knew it. Anyway, I turned on the radio and that's when I heard Grover Washington for the first time. Songs like *Trouble Man, Mercy Mercy Me (The Ecology), Mister Magic* and *Georgia On My Mind* were signature pieces with all kinds of ranges and runs.

I never knew this kind of music. Of course, I didn't tell Mom and Dad because you were not supposed to listen to anything but Church music. *Until It's Time for You to Go* was smooth and deliberate. However, as time went by, there were pieces like *Knucklehead* and *Feels So Good* that were loaded with such spirited creativity it made me wonder about our attention to music in the Church. Why am I saying all of this?

We should be happy in the Church and put all of our energy, creativity and everything we've got into our music to lift up the Lord. These guys used their talent bringing it to the secular world.

I could not play the saxophone freely at any given time in the house. I could not play like I wanted around the school. I could not play freely at church. It felt like I could not play the saxophone anywhere! Unlike in the secular world, there are no guilds or "night spots" down the street for Christian instrumentalists to go hang out and learn from the best. What kid wouldn't give up on the dream? It was important to find good sources of inspiration and encouragement that would help inspire me. Some of that came through listening to people like Coltrane, Charlie Parker and Michael Brecker.

Now don't misunderstand. Gamble Gade had a lot of groups when I was growing up as child. Groups like the Sunshine Sisters, the Twilights, the Starlights, Gospel Tones, Gospel Singers, Prophecy Brothers and the Virgin Island Gospel Ensemble – they were rocking and had a lot of youthful energy. Now with people like Washington and other technical artists, we could capitalize on these external influences to help raise the level of our instrumentation and arrangements.

One of our saxophonists, Mario Todman, was a genius. He played everything – guitar, bass, steel drums – you name it. My eyes and ears were always stretched wide open when I heard him play. I can still hear his arrangement on the sax playing, "Jesus is Coming Soon." I am happy to say that he was impressed with me as I was coming up. The Starlights, was also one of my favorites. Playing with the Starlights was the highlight of my earliest experiences because we approached every musical piece as if we were on a journey, and packed every program with powerful message songs as if our music was a lifeline to the throne of mercy. We put everything we had into our playing and raised the roof when we praised God. It was just a few of us, including Cecil Jones, Jason Fahie, and Herbert Coakley. We had the two saxophones, one trumpet and a drummer. We were only 12-13 years old, but oh, we were excited, and we handled our business for the Lord. Those were the days and I still cherish them.

As I look back over my life and think where I came from and where I am now, I realize just how good the Lord has been to me. I am thankful that as tough as my days have been, I am who God made me to be. A lot of expressions of appreciation are reflected in my saxophone.

Miles Davis once said, "You can tell the history of jazz in four words: Louis Armstrong. Charlie Parker." Wouldn't it be nice if God's people would honor the gift He has given us that we would become excellent for the kingdom of God?

On Sunday morning I would bring my saxophone to the church, and while I was playing the Pastor would say from the pulpit, "Son, don't play." Feeling sad, I would lay my saxophone down and hang my head in embarrassment. Sometimes those words landed on my chest like a ton of bricks.

During this time many singers and instrumental groups in the church and other churches in the area were searching for musicians, especially saxophone players. I expressed my interest in playing with these groups, but they would turn me down.

One Saturday afternoon when I arrived at rehearsal, even before I entered the room, there was laughter from the other band members. I continued to assemble my saxophone and the laughter got even louder. Although I was crying on the inside, I kept my composure saying to myself, "I will take it like a man."

After rehearsal had ended, I disassembled my horn and started walking home. While heading home I began to cry really hard. I felt so bad about the way I was being treated for not being good on my horn. Now for all of you who are going through something in your life. Understand this. This was my breaking point. It was like one of those situations where you say either God is coming down here to fix it or you are going up there where He is (in heaven) to fix it. This is when no man on the earth can fix what is wrong. Then is when you need the Almighty God from heaven. He is the only One that can heal you.

So I prayed to God at that very moment and said "Lord, if YOU teach me to play this horn real good, I will only play this saxophone to your Glory and Honor until the day I leave this present world.

From that moment on, I knew I was meant to play the saxophone – no matter how bad I sounded then. I just knew that no matter what, I was going to be a saxophonist. A typical day for me was just like that of the other boys except one difference. I just spent a lot of intimate time with God on that horn. No matter how bad I sounded – and even if it was just for 5 or 10 minutes a day. That time was between me and God. Even if someone tried to toss me off a cliff or over side of a mountain, I was going to keep a grip and play that saxophone all the way down the slopes.

I even felt connected to the saxophone's creator. Adolphe Sax, a Belgian clarinetist and flutist, became obsessed when he recognized an imbalance in orchestras, noting that the brass instruments overwhelmed the woodwinds, while the woodwinds drowned out the strings. His father, Belgium's head instrument maker, had the right connections so Adolphe was able to create an instrument to level out the quality of sound between the timbre of the clarinet and the power of the trumpet.

Despite anger and jealousy among other instrument makers, the theft of some of his patented designs, lawsuits filed against him and several attempts made on his life, Sax survived and so did the sensual timbre of his saxophone. It was a good thing he did not get discouraged when people ridiculed him for making the instrument. His enemies likened the S-curve of the sax to the undulating curves of a dancing woman, and when played by particular musicians, they relegated the sound to that of some mystical power which seduced its listeners. Of course, critics seized this opportunity to popularize their opinions and carelessly associated the instrument with sin, making it an easy target and effectively banning it from religious music. The saxophone made its way to the United States through New Orleans, where it was first introduced into the underground "jazz" sound emerging in nightclubs in early 1910. Although criticized heavily for its throaty sound, the hardness began to wear off and later the saxophone became quite a hit in itself. Eventually, other plaintive instrument companies began producing their own saxophones! His competitors had tormented him so badly that even Sax was beginning to question the beauty of such a wonderful gift. If not for him, we would not have the sounds of such artist greats like Coltrane, Brecker, "Bird" Parker and Grover Washington. If he had given up, I would not be a saxophonist today!

Now I did not understand all of these mature themes during my teens. I just knew that the saxophone hit me real hard somewhere deep inside. I really loved my dad back then, too, because he seemed to understand. Somehow, deep inside, I think he got me. Nobody else seemed to notice when things were going on deep inside me but my dad could always sense or feel my distress. Sometimes he would come up to me, look me square in the eyes, with his heavy voice and say, "Son, you've got something no one else has. You are gifted." There were just a few words here or there, but that was enough to boost my confidence and to still any doubt or fear. I had no idea until this season of my life, just how much his love for me would take me through life. He never once discouraged me. I will never forget.

One Friday afternoon, I got thrown out of the 8th grade band class by the Music Teacher, Mr. Eric Christian. I wasn't hitting my notes right and everything was off with me. I simply wasn't feeling it. Quite frankly, I was still struggling. Mr. Christian was also a Baptist Choir Director and great musician in his own right, but I sure didn't like getting thrown out especially since he knew my father. In fact, almost everybody on the Island knew Dad because at that time, he worked at the largest SuperMarket on the Island.

It so happened that we had a Singspiration at our Church on that very Sunday. Their Choir was the Guest Choir. When we pulled to Gamble Gade, there was Mr. Christian, standing right outside. Man, was I scared. I dropped my head a little and waited. Then I heard my father, ask, "So, how's my son doing on the saxophone?" I waited, holding my breath. Mr. Christian answered, "Oh, Ira? He's doing great, just great." Whew! I escaped that one. I thought he was going to tell my Dad he threw me out of the class on Friday. I owed Mr. Christian big time for that one. I really wanted to make my father proud.

At church, other things were happening. Although I wasn't so good while Bishop Finlayson was there, years later when I bumped into him stateside, he heard me play. He made me feel good, expressing admiration for my touch on the saxophone. His words of praise erased the past – well, most of it. It actually felt real good. It felt like I had redeemed myself!

The Church did well under Bishop Finlayson. In fact, he put the Church of God of Prophecy on the map. He was the first to invite USVI dignitaries, officials and people of high ranking government representatives to our territorial conventions. It was then that the COGOP received proper exposure and people really began to learn about the Church. When he came the church was not very well known, but because of his articulation, the establishment of the choir that sang at a lot of major events, the church received recognition all over the Caribbean. On top of that, the new overseer had an uncanny knack for people and a strong sense of belonging. He was a natural and he fit right in with the natives. He was called upon to speak, render musical selections and represent the church at a lot of functions on the islands. It was because of this man of God that I took up the saxophone and never put it down again.

Bishop Finlayson served in this capacity from 1971 to 1975, at which time he became the General Field Secretary to the General Overseer. He also served as an instructor at the Bible Training Institute of the schools located in Cleveland, Fullerton, California, Jamaica, British West Indies, Manila, Philippines and the British and U.S. Virgin Islands. The ordination charged him with great responsibility and authority. What happened next was clearly by divine appointment.

Sometimes I think back on the days back home. I can see my sisters and my brother all gathered out on the porch with my brother strumming, "The Great Speckled Bird." Naomi and Ruth would sing along in harmony. I never could quite match their skills but they never made me feel bad. I can hear my dad's trombone voice. Mom would sometimes sing along with us. I would hum. I loved my family.

It's like the flower bushes outside. She brought the brightness and beauty of the flower garden into our home. We were all a part of her garden. Life has changed in a lot of ways now that Mom, Dad and Naomi are gone. I miss those days and I miss my sister Naomi dearly. Naomi was my big sister and was always there for me. When she left this world, I was truly hurt. My fondest memories of her are how I could easily play pranks on her. I did it all the time. She would prank me back but she wasn't so good at it although she did know how to "jack me up" when she'd had just about enough of me as they would say. No one had to tell me – I knew for myself that she loved me. Those were all good memories for always.

Chapter 4

Fostering a Determined, Made Up Mind

Stay focused and stay determined. Don't look to anyone else to be your determination - have self-determination. It will take you very far.

Justice Smith

The Brass Band was finally ready to play for the Church of God of Prophecy Annual Convention. The air was abuzz with excitement as the band gathered. In fact, this was a high time for the entire Church in the Virgin Islands and especially exhilarating for me because I would be performing for the first time in a parade. Somehow, I felt qualified, significant and had a sense of belonging.

Even more exciting for me was discovering that the Bahamas Brass Band from the Church of God of Prophecy in Nassau, Bahamas would be performing along with us. This was no small event. The Bahama Brass Band is an internationally¬ acclaimed gospel music institution of the Church of God of Prophecy. Established in 1925, the world renowned band has lifted up the name of Jesus Christ around the world through its highly spirited music.

To be a part of the newly established US Virgin Islands Brass Band had already given me quite a thrill, but to be able to march with the Bahama Brass Band set me in high gear. This band has played before Kings and the Rulers of the earth and here I was, marching among great musicians who served before royalty and performed for years at the Church of God of Prophecy local, state and annual worldwide functions. I was just a beginner and yet here I was, walking among these pillars of fire! This was not just a group of musicians but rather an institution of selfless, dedicated soldiers marching for God. Just thinking about it stirs up all kinds of emotions that I cannot describe. Marching with them was like being in God's army, a force not to be contended with on any day. This was a gift.

The parade route was about three quarters of a mile from the Lionel Roberts Stadium to the Moravian Church. We were dressed in black and white with red vests. It was a tremendous honor for our Brass Band to march at the front of the parade with the Bahamas Brass Band marching at the rear. That amazing performance of the first songs I learned to play on my saxophone *Who Is On the Lord's Side*, and *Onward Christian Soldiers,* became one of the highlights of my saxophone experiences. Just being a part of the band had a personal impact on me. Whereas before I may have been somewhat nervous and a little overwhelmed, I eventually become confident and well adjusted. I believe playing a musical instrument contributed to my leadership skills, tenacity and made me a team player. This is how we evolve into true leaders who lead with confidence, setting the example and losing our egos in the process.

The USVI Brass Band remained in existence for approximately one and a half years. During this time I would practice my horn everyday for at least 45 minutes at school. On Saturday's, I practiced a minimum of one and a half hours at band practice and at home. I also played during morning and evening services at church. This pattern lasted for years. God continued to touch me greatly and gave me the mindset to practice as much as possible.

I became increasingly interested in gospel music and began listening to more contemporary gospel artists. I really loved the group Andraé Crouch and The Disciples who came out of the COGIC (Church of God in Christ). Crouch, whose father was a street preacher, was most widely recognized as the first black gospel artist to appeal to both religious and secular audiences across multiracial lines.

Crouch's music inspired me because he had several great saxophone players performing solos in some of his songs. Some of his band rocked, in the rock 'n' roll sense rather than in the gospel tradition but he was clearly a little before his time. His earlier traditional tunes like his first album *The Blood Will Never Lose its Power, Through it All, and My Tribute (To God Be the Glory)* have captivated his audiences for years. Crouch had Michael Brecker, prolific jazz saxophonist and composer, playing instrumental solo. Acknowledged as a quiet, gentle musician widely regarded as the most influential tenor saxophonist since John Coltrane, Brecker was totally technical and was actually one of my favorites.

As Couch's music became more progressive, it became a challenge for me to try and play these saxophone parts. I would practice even harder to achieve or measure up to the skills of his musicians. It was not easy, but I acquired better improvisational skills. Brecker was diagnosed with a bone marrow disease and died in January 2007 at age 57. Even though he was on his last legs with leukemia, he remained in demand right up until the end, completing his last album just two short weeks before his death. Such legends left quite an impression on me. Even those that were not part of the gospel industry were impressive. For example, jazz saxophonist Grover Washington, Jr. was an accomplished musician by age 12. One of the most popular saxophonists of all time, he was the pacesetter in his field and most prominent jazz musician living in Philadelphia. He collapsed on stage after taping a performance for "The Saturday Early Show" at the CBS studio in Manhattan and died at age 56. Charlie "The Bird" Parker was brilliant in terms of his runs – no one could touch him. To this day, more than 40 years after his death, he was only 34 years old, Bird remains jazz's single most venerated figure.

By 1975, I had been playing the saxophone for almost a year. Many of the groups who previously did not want me to play with their bands were now beginning to reach out to me and were now inquiring about the change in my playing. They had observed a difference in my playing ability. Some of the guys began to ask me, "What happened to you? You are sounding different." I looked at them somberly. My mind flashed back to what seemed to be many years ago.

"It's a secret that I will tell you in years to come," I quietly replied. Inside, I felt very calm. The Lord was with me.

Bishop Rhymer. Once again, a new Territorial Overseer to the United States and British Virgin Islands was appointed by General Headquarters Church of God of Prophecy. Bishop Rueben R. Rhymer, a native of the British Virgin Islands, had migrated to the United States at an early age. He came to the Virgin Islands with six sons. Four of them were musicians. To me, Bishop Rhymer already had his congregation. The brothers were very talented and gifted musicians. They were a welcome addition to No. 20 Gamble Gade. In addition, they were young and we connected well. The year 1975 was an exciting time for me. One of the more notable reasons was that the local Church of God of Prophecy church at No. 20 Gamble Gade had produced a new group by the name of The Gospel Tones.

The Gospel Tones. The Gospel Tones was a tightly knitted group because a lot of the members were brothers. The band was comprised of a keyboard player *(Samuel Rhymer)*, bass guitar player *(Edwin Vanterpool)*, two trumpet players *(Cecil Jones and Raymond Rhymer)*, one clarinet player *(Rudel Rhymer),* two saxophone players *(Leonardo Jacobs and me)*, two trombone players *(Verdell Turnbull and Berchard Jacobs),* one drummer *(Verlin Turnbull)* and Congo player *(Willie Vasquez)* and a synthesizer player *(Russell Jones)*. The band had to make use of a temporary guitar player (Keith Fahie) since we did not have a permanent one but I loved playing in this band for a lot of reasons. First, I was young and had great opportunities to travel and bless God and others with my talents and gifts. Secondly, I was working with many members of the band who had teased me mercilessly during the brass band era because I could not play.

Have you ever witnessed a miracle? Well, I want you to witness a miracle from God in my life. The Gospel Tones had a theme song entitled Bridge Over Trouble Waters. The featured soloist was none other than the saxophonist that everyone had scoffed, laughed at and mocked: Me!

The scripture clearly states "If God be for us, who can be against us?" God was definitely working in my life. There was a lot of excitement and anticipation in this band. We played for parades, banquets, concerts, many church functions, and we traveled throughout the British and United States Virgin Islands. We were the featured gospel band and had it going on. By this time, I had been playing for approximately three years. I desperately wanted a new saxophone because the Martin alto saxophone, which was an older horn, had a lot of mechanical issues.

Working to replace my Sax. My parents and I came up with the idea of how to raise funds to purchase this new saxophone. The idea that we came up with was to obtain a newspaper route and to wash my neighbor's cars to raise funds. I chose The Virgin Islands Home Journal Newspaper Company based in Contant the west part of St. Thomas, because my first cousin, Kenneth Christopher, was the owner.

My newspaper route consisted of walking from the Contant area to my neighborhood, in the Estate Thomas community, which was about 2.0 miles but it felt like 5.0 miles to me. The cost of the newspaper was about 10 cents a copy. This route was an adventurous one. I had to walk through the middle of a mysterious old cemetery, slightly hidden in a woody area with tall trees. The site was fairly large for a teenager to walk during late evenings—about a half acre—with only the moon and stars to offer any lighting. Someone said old cemeteries are referred to as "thin" places—places where the veil separating two worlds is translucent.

One night while walking through the cemetery, my mind started to play tricks on me. I imagined that I was seeing and hearing things that did not exist. A shiver ran up my spine. The words "Ashes to ashes, dust to dust" formed in my mind. I thought I heard the clanking of shovels against stone and the thud of earth being thrown on coffin lids. I imagined the creaky wheels of a wagon bearing down on me. I walked faster. I thought I heard a dog barking. Then it made a deep throaty, growling noise. It might have been my imagination but, I dropped a lot of the newspapers that night! One time I came around the bend near the end of the cemetery just in time to see the sunken shadow of a ghostly mother's arm clutching her children as they glided right past me. I was never so frighten in my life.

For nearly 15 months I served the newspapers. Although I cannot describe what went through my mind as I stared at those elongated sunken grave areas or how afraid I was when I sensed the hot breath of a stinking dog on my face, I do believe my heart grew braver because I endured the test. I could only do this by the grace of God. Despite the stab of fear that came over me and the many times I thought I was being chased down by that big smelly dog, I was determined more than ever to stick it out until I could get my new saxophone. In hindsight, it occurred to me that God was building my character and endurance.

By then, Bishop Rhymer's tenure was over. He and his family relocated to Houston, Texas. The Gospel Tones was disbanded around the summer of 1978. This was tough for me because my life was now music and these guys had become family. Most of them had graduated from high school and quite naturally, life must go on but I would truly miss those days with the Gospel Tones.

Bishop Rogers. Once again, the COGOP appointed a new territorial Overseer by the name of Rufus R. Rogers to the Virgin Islands.

It was another wonderful experience and I was particularly thankful that Bishop Roger's wife, Sister Verona, was an outstanding pianist who played with originality and depth, bringing the Christian message to life in extraordinary ways. Therefore the music did not stop in the Virgin Islands. She worked enthusiastically to keep the music flowing fluently in the church. We continued to perform at conventions, and the local church at No. 20 Gamble Gade and C-5 Hoffman, the COGOP U.S.V.I./B.V.I. Territorial Church Headquarters. In addition to working with the band, I now performed with the Virgin Islands Church of God Of Prophecy mass choir.

Moving to New York. I spent my grammar school years wishing to spread my wings and fly away like the little sparrow – completely unrestricted – and now that senior high school was over, the time had come. Decisions had to be made. Although education is critical; a four-year college degree is not. Besides, college is not for everyone. I was not quite ready to take that path. In 1980, after completing high school, I relocated to the mainland USA in Queens, New York and attended The Church of God of Prophecy in Bronx, New York. This was a big change for me coming from an island that is about 35 square miles and moving to the big state of New York. Queens, the easternmost and largest area of the five boroughs of New York City, is the most ethnically diverse urban area in the world. Famous as the home of the Yankee Stadium, the Bronx is also the greenest of New York City's boroughs. This was going to be a big, exciting adventure. I continued to praise and worship the Lord with my music, playing in various groups.

Performing with the New York state COGOP Brass Band under the direction of Deacon Allen Smith was one of the first big opportunities that allowed me get involved. A different set of challenges were introduced when I went to New York. The music to which I'd become accustomed to in the Virgin Islands, was based on a Caribbean style, which reflects different genres of long-standing West Indian cultural ties to the island nations to the south. However, the Christian music in New York was totally different from the music in the Virgin Islands. Though there were different genres, it was primarily gospel. Much of it was contemporary music, which is composed and performed for many purposes, including aesthetic pleasure, religious or ceremonial purposes, and for entertainment, all usually with dominant harmonized vocals. It trended toward an urban flow, attracting a diverse audience. It was a segue into mainstream secular music. I had a chance to let the Spirit of the Lord use me in the music ministry.

The Bronx COGOP was a great church to attend and a beautiful church in which to play. I was privileged to meet some great musicians during this period and acquired a great deal of knowledge from some of the church musicians. Brothers John Henry, *(keyboardist)*; Clayton Harris *(alto saxophonist)*, and Alfredo Anthony *(drummer)* were some of the Bronx's finest. They were all exceptionally gifted and men of character.

Playing in the Bronx church change my style of playing. Initially, I was treated like a stepchild, but the musicians quickly found out that I was blessed by God with my playing. They embraced and welcomed me to attend. Soon I was playing at conventions and different functions. My talent was being exposed but it was God who was glorified.

Bishop Rogers was a genuine, enthusiastic encourager. He liked to hear me play. It was because of his influence that I was able to participate in the New York Project 2001. However, there were a lot of negative vibes and jealousy stemming from people who did not know or understand me or my style of playing. I am a natural at giving all I have to praise the Lord on my instrument.

People can be very discouraging sometimes. I didn't really want to do anymore projects because I felt I had to tone down my playing so as to not offend anyone. When I was asked to play "Center of My Joy" at a live performance in the Bronx Church, my heart was not in it as it normally would be. The piece wasn't to my satisfaction and I had to return to the studio. When I had to return to the studio a second time at Sister Verona's request, I hesitated. This was during a period that I was struggling financially. Yet I knew I needed to do the piece right so I agreed.

This time, I didn't hold back. The producer was shocked. The song was so in-depth and crazy-like amazing. If you understand what I am saying, it is simply this – the anointing was upon me and it was as though my mind was in another world. They had to cut it up it was so heavy and technical. There were not a lot of runs – it was simply in four of five dimensions. For an alto saxophone, you would not believe it was possible! They wanted to use the piece at a wedding but it was too technical so they cut it up,

This particular performance recording brought exposure and glorified God. I knew that I had held back the first time because of the jealousy and not wanting to make enemies but the next time, I just focused on God. After that, people went "crazy" and began to call me Ira "Scatman".

The worst thing about the whole situation was that everyone had practiced and knew how the piece was to be done but I had not practiced with the group. Neither did anyone explain to me how the piece was to be done so when it was time, I simply brought it full force! Somehow, they loved it.

As I reflect back on these times, it is clear that I did not really understand the great gift that God have given to me. During those days, I did many different jobs but I should have concentrated on playing the horn "full time" and understanding my worth. I worked for a rental car company and the owners entrusted me with the tasks of handling the cash box and opening up the store but when I proposed to become business partners with them, they did not want me. I began thinking about taking my life seriously and about making myself available to the Lord. Then one day I said, "I quit this job." My cousin, Barbara Foy, kept telling me to join the army but I said I wanted to join a branch of service that is different.

Joining the Coast Guard. The United States Coast Guard is an elite force that values integrity and that rewards excellence. They tell you that every job you perform is significant and everything you do will be noticed. In April of 1982, I joined the U.S. Coast Guard branch. It's famous "Make a difference on land, sea or in the air" pitch attracted my attention. The Coast Guard Academy is the only federal military academy that does not require a Congressional appointment, and admission is strictly on the basis of the Scholastic Aptitude Test and consideration of extracurricular involvement. In 1973 28 Black cadets were sworn in. In 1974 20 Black cadets were admitted as part of the Class of 1978. In the early 1980's, the first African American female joined. I am bringing up these statistics because in recent years, I have heard that the Coast Guard is notorious for racism, more so than the other branches of the military; and this is from Caucasian and minority members. I did not understand the implications of these numbers until much later. The United States Coast Guard Academy graduated their first African-American Cadet in 1966. Prior to 1962, only one African-American Cadet, Javis Wright, had been admitted. Based on my experience, I cringe at the thought of what he probably endured.

It was billionaire Ray Dalio, who once said *"Success comes from knowing what you don't know, more than coming from what you do know."*

The Coast Guard was a challenging career, but I never stop playing my saxophone. While attending the Coast Guard boot camp, I tried to become a member of the marching band, but was unsuccessful. Never before had the pressure to perform been so intense nor had any particular curriculum meant so much for my academic future as in the Coast Guard.

I found comfort in God and through playing my saxophone. I knew I had to praise God regardless of the stress I experienced. God says, "Whoever offers praise glorifies Me; and to him who orders his conduct aright I will show the salvation of God." *(Psalm 50:23)* This verse is a constant reminder of why we should praise the Lord. My praise was in accordance with that Bible verse and in reflection of the 150th Psalm. Praise God!

The sailors would hear me practicing and would often challenge me to see if I could play a song. I would play a lot of times for them when we had free time.

Auditioning to become a member of the Coast Guard band based in New London, Connecticut was a painful experience. The pressure to do well is always there, but for some reason, this particular season was significant to me. Part of me wanted to prove to myself that I was good enough; the other part of me wanted to make my folks proud. Of course, you do everything possible to prepare and then the day finally comes. My stomach was churning as usual. I confess that I was sleep-deprived and a little miserable. Like any kind of human behavior, the response to competitive pressure is derived from a complex set of factors: *how we were raised, our skills and experience, the talents and our natural tendencies.* However, God kept and brought me out of that turmoil!

Understanding stress factors and how to deal with situations can help people compete. However, stress is far more complicated than previously assumed. Unlike long-term stress, short-term stress can actually help people perform better and viewing it that way changes its effect. Even for those genetically predisposed to anxiety, the answer is not necessarily less competition — it's more competition. It just needs to be the right kind.

In learning how to use stress in a productive way, I made a video of me playing a variety of different songs. One of my choices of songs was the Coast Guard song that I remembered hearing from boot camp.

I put everything into perfecting that song so that I would be selected for membership. When the results came back, I was informed that this was not a jazz band and should therefore consider another band to join. They did not offer any substantive suggestions or hopeful advice about future audition possibilities. There was no positive feedback or consideration of any kind. It was very cold. They were telling me in so many words, "We do not want you."

This was a big disappointment – in fact, it was the worst. It was a low feeling because the band was predominately white and I was African American. To dismiss me or treat me as if I was unworthy of serious consideration was like a slap in the face. At this point, I began some serious thinking and knew I must realize my worth. I had devoted four years of my life to the United States Coast Guard and during this time, I had not become a band member and did not get promoted. Yet, I continued to believe, praise and worship God.

This was absolutely critical to my peace of mind for what I needed to do. Serving God is very serious and one must be sincere in the daily pursuit of Him. This was not optional; I knew I must praise Him every day. For example, I practiced intensely while stationed on the Coast Guard Cutter Point Wells ship in Montauk, New York, a Long Island town. I was the first African American to be stationed on this vessel since it had been assigned to The Coast Guard Station at Montauk, in 1961. That speaks volumes. The 82-footer has since been decommissioned on October 13, 2000 after 36 years of service and replaced by another ship.

One day when I was scheduled to perform my duty or security watch, I was practicing on the outside deck of the ship. A couple who was sitting in their car, observed me practicing.

The gentleman stepped out of his car started walking towards the boat. He called out, "My wife and I were sitting in the car checking out your playing. We really like the way you play that saxophone!"

He also stated that he would love for me to come and play with his band in the town area. "I am the owner of the club in Montauk. You sure would enhance my band. If you are interested, I will pay you very well, and you can play when you are off duty. You sure do have the skills to make my band sound good."

"Sir, I do not play that type of music," I replied quietly.

He did not get the message. He said, "We heard you playing and we have no doubt you know how to play that type of music."

As I shook my head slowly, appreciating the attention, I realized I needed to make myself very clear.

"If it is secular music, I cannot do it, because it would be against my religious principles to play that type of music in a club setting. If it is not religious type music I will not play it," I responded.

There, I thought. That should be enough to make him marvel. Perhaps it would help him at how one can be committed to God. I had made a covenant with God and cannot break it. I did not tell him what the covenant was; I just stated that I could not do it.

The man did not receive my refusal very well. He walked away shaking his head in unbelief and telling his wife, "This guy is crazy."

Having made a serious commitment to God, I vaguely explained that I must honor an agreement I had made and that deviating from that principle would result in my not being able to play under the anointing nor at a heightened inspired level.

Very much like the enemy, the man was only interested in his agenda. As he walked away, he kept looking back at me wondering how I could turn down such a lucrative opportunity. What he did not understand was my oath, my commitment to God, was between the Lord and I; it could not be broken.

During this time, I was flat broke but though I had no money, I fully trusted God and replied flatly but firmly, "No!"

When I was off duty, I traveled to New York City from Long Island New York to minister in music at revivals and other religious functions. Praising God on the saxophone is what I really desired and loved to do. This was my passion. Psalm 150:1:6 states "Praise ye the Lord, Praise God in his sanctuary. Praise him in the firmament of his power. Praise him for his mighty acts: Praise him according to his excellent greatness. Praise him with the sound of the trumpet: Praise him with the Psaltery and harp: Praise him with the timbrel and dance. Praise him with string instruments and organs. Praise him upon the loud cymbals: Praise him upon high sounding Cymbals. Let everything that have breathe praise the Lord praise ye the Lord!" This was my daily living before God; I would not trade this time with God for anything.

Bishop Felix Garcia, a field secretary from The Church of God of Prophecy in Cleveland, Tennessee was a representative for one of our New York state Church of God of Prophecy conventions. When he heard about the Malta Street Church's group by the name of The Chariot Inspires, he invited us to minister at the COGOP General Assembly in Cleveland, Tennessee in 1984. I originally played the drums for this group because they were in desperate need of a drummer so I put down my saxophone and volunteered to play for them. God eventually sent a drummer, named Roger Knight, who unfortunately passed away within a few months of writing this book, and I went back to playing my saxophone. There is a part of me that wants to testify about how God does things so only He gets the credit.

Those who knew Roger personally will join with me in praising God that when I passed the drumsticks on to Roger, we eon saw a definite work of grace in his life as he played those drums. There is no comparison to how God orchestrates everything. Had I been selfish and held on to playing the drums, the change that was needed might never have occurred. I believe God is at work in us to will and do His good pleasure. I am certain that it was no coincident that I was invited and therefore, ministered with joy on the alto saxophone at the General Assembly the very next year. If I had held selfishly onto playing drums, it is likely that I would never have received that blessing from the Lord!

Departing the Military. April of 1986 was a huge moment in my life for this is when I was honorably discharged from the United States Coast Guard. I did not have any plans at this time, and although I was not sad to leave, it was still with mixed emotions that I departed. One thing I knew without doubt, was that I was glad to leave the Armed Forces.

My childhood friend, Amos Carty, Jr., a Howard university student, asked me, "Scat" (that is my nickname), "Where are you going? And what are you planning to do now that you are discharged from the Coast Guard?"

Without hesitation, I said the first thing that came to mind. "Maybe I will go to Miami, Florida!" Inwardly I was thinking about a young lady down there that I liked, but the Father knows best.

Amos replied," Why don't you come to Washington, DC? It is a military orientated area and since you are honorably discharged, you should be able to acquire a job easily." I rolled these thoughts over in my mind and apparently, I didn't respond quickly enough.

He said, "Hey, don't worry about anything. You can stay with me until you get a job and get on your feet."

I took Amos up on his offer and relocated to Washington. It was going to be a challenge coming to an unfamiliar place with no job, very little money, and only a car filled with everything that I owned. Worse, I had nothing but a bunch of credit cards in my pocket and had to stand on the merit of a childhood friend's promise.

I will never forget my friend Amos. This was quite a serious situation. I had to keep one thing in mind: *Praising and worshiping God comes with focused commitment, determination and understanding.* Every time we give God praise, something happens in the spiritual ream. The question is what we really want to see as a result of our worship. I still believed God but did not understand my musical worth. The scripture clearly states God is a spirit and they that worship him must worship him in spirit and in truth. I knew I must stay focused. I had to trust God that something would work out for my life in Washington, D.C.

Praising and worshiping God breaks the bands of the enemy, it breaks chains and bondages and it looses shackles. When I take my saxophone to the highest level in ministering to God's people, I always strive to make sure that the focus is on and about Him. With this concept in my mind and in everything I do, the Lord can receive the glory and honor.

I refused to be distracted, no matter the situation or how uncertain a situation seemed. Through troubles, trials and disappointments, I knew I must consistently worship Him. The ultimate goal is to bring freedom in expressive adoration to the Lord.

Moving to Washington, DC. Practicing and staying efficient with my playing was what I continued to do. When I began attending The Church of God Of Prophecy on Capitol Hill in Washington, D.C., I was delighted. The pastor of the church was Bishop John C. Newkirk, a former COGOP worldwide Evangelist. The first Sunday that I attended services and played my saxophone, the congregants received me very well. I knew I was going to be happy and blessed at this church because Bishop Newkirk was a dynamic preacher and I loved powerful preaching.

This church had some magnificent musicians who were quite talented. They performed exceptionally well playing their instruments. The amazing thing was that most of the musicians were relatives comprised of the West and Lee families (Jeffrey West was impressive on the keys; the rest were proficient at everything they did and all of them were humble). Their families were headed by the most loving endearing people I know. Jan Jones became my big sister and encourager; and without Mother Lee, the matriarch of the family, I wouldn't have felt so welcome in her home every Sunday. These two families treated me like family, regularly inviting me to their home with my childhood friend Amos to make sure we had plenty to eat and drink. This was greatly appreciated. I played on Sunday mornings with the Lee singers and the church choir directed by Brother Ted Scotton. These talented musicians had a different style of music.

Once again, I found myself changing my style of music slightly. I had a lot of fun playing with these musicians but it was very challenging. These musicians inspired me to take my music to a different level.

God gave me another opportunity to praise and worship Him again with a different style of music. I subsequently became very involved playing for many solo artists and groups. Sister Joan Foster, Capitol Hill Church musician and Voices of Praise choir pianist, accompanied some of my solos and was a great supporter. I ministered at the Capitol Hill church from the summer of 1986 to the beginning of the year 1995. During this time I enrolled at the Northern Virginia community College on Alexandria campus to enhance my musical skills, and to increase my playing proficiency.

Attending this college give me the opportunity to play my saxophone in the Jazz ensemble and the concert band. I was selected many times to perform various jazz solos on the alto saxophone. One of the pieces that I was featured as a soloist was Norwegian Woods. Being one of the few African Americans in the band was fortuitous and provided me the unexpected opportunity to demonstrate my improved playing, technical skills and relevance, especially in the style of African American cultural music.

I was always happy and eager to spread the good news about Jesus Christ to others and to anyone with whom I come in contact. I love telling them about salvation and how God has blessed me with a musical talent, skills and his anointing on my life to play the tenor saxophone.

DC ARMY National Guard. In April 1988 I became a member of the District of Columbia United States Army National Guard in Washington, DC. As a reservist, my specialty Military Occupational Specialty was 71 Mike, Chaplain's Assistant. This was one of the best jobs I have ever held. Performing in this capacity allowed me to help soldiers to experience and see that God really exists. This opportunity to minister was enormous. By introducing them to the gospel, I was able to show them, according to Scripture, that God is a rewarder of those who diligently seek Him. While ministering to the soldiers at religious services, I was praising and worship God on my saxophone.

God was faithful in opening many doors. I ministered constantly to the soldiers. Since I was an enlisted member and not an officer, many of the soldiers felt very comfortable confiding in me. I was required to attend training and drill one weekend every month and to attend a 2-weeks training session once a year. Sometimes while performing the weekend drills, I would take about 45 minutes away from the National Guard Armory and go to the Capitol Hill Church of God of Prophecy church service, for praise and worship, and then return to the Armory. This was possible because the church was not too far from the Armory.

Ministering to these broken soldiers brought a deep joy to me. To institutionalize the ministry, I implemented a special project called "Thought for the Day", which consisted of posting Scriptures throughout the Armory facility. I did this so that as the troops performed their daily missions and tasks, they will see the scriptures posted and be spiritually uplifted.

Losing my Yahama Alto Model 61 Saxophone. In February of 1990, my sister Naomi Donaldson, who lived in Queens, New York went home to be with the Lord. This was a devastating time for my family. Three months prior to her death her husband Minister David Donaldson passed away. Naomi's passing was very difficult for me. She was only 35 years old. She took good care of me when I moved to the New York City from the US Virgin Island. I really loved her a lot. That's what an older sister would do for her younger brother but not all people would do that. Naomi was my confidant and my friend. To this day, I still miss her quirky smile and her gentle laughter. In honor of her memory, I think someday I will compose and dedicate a song to her.

Naomi had such a warm spirit. She was a quiet person who didn't mess with anyone. One night, a few years after she had passed away, she came to me in a dream. In the dream she was dressed in the white dress that she was buried in. She asked me, "Why is everyone crying for me?"

I said everyone was sad because you died at such a young age. She replied, "Remember I was your sister when I was on the earth." Then she finished, "Tell everyone: Don't cry for me because I am safe!" I blinked my eyes and she was gone.

Naomi had one daughter named Sabrina Donaldson. She was in the custody of her paternal grandmother in Youngstown, Ohio after her parents passed. Sabrina was only 10 years old when her parents passed.

My family depended on me to make the arrangements for Naomi's body to be shipped to the US Virgin Islands. Several things had to be done in order for this trip to be made. While I was making the arrangements and communicating with my family on these things, I was also dealing with my niece, Sabrina and trying to keep myself together. A great weight was upon my shoulders and it felt like I aged overnight. The whole family was going through the pain of it all but I felt very much alone in so many ways. There were so many details and the stress only compounded things, making my grief almost unbearable.

Confronted with so many issues and with feelings raging inside, I knew I needed God to help me. When the time arrived, I drove from my home in the state of Maryland to Youngstown, Ohio to pick up my niece Sabrina and immediately returned to Maryland. Sabrina and I prepared to travel to the US Virgin Islands. We flew from Maryland to New York City.

Once we arrived in New York, I was very concerned about Sabrina who had become very sick on the flight so we hastily exited the plane. In my hurry to unload, I forgot to retrieve my saxophone from the overhead compartment. Once I realized that I had forgotten my horn, I hurried back to report that my horn was left on the plane but was told by the airline agent that the plane had already departed for Philadelphia, Pennsylvania. She also commented, "Oh my husband plays the saxophone!"

It has been 26 years and the saxophone has never been returned. I was devastated about the loss of this saxophone that meant so much to me. I had worked very hard selling newspapers as a young boy to purchase my horn, and now it was gone after having it for 13 years. It was such horrible feeling of emptiness and dread; I kept hoping it was only a dream.

Prior to traveling the night before, I cleaned out the saxophone case and threw out several old papers. Now there was no long an address or other personal information inside the case. For approximately 10 years I moped around every day. I was so hurt about the loss of my saxophone. I never really got over the loss; I simply learned to live with the loss. I always wonder what happened to it. Did someone else play it? Did the power of the anointing bless anyone? I continue to hope that one day, it will be returned to me. It was such an intimate part of me. To lose my sister and on top of that, my Yamaha alto saxophone 361, was the worst of worst.

Long Awaited Reward in DC. I was 26 years of age, but my mind was still young to the point after having many female friends I met a young lady while attending Capitol Hill Church of God of Prophecy. She was attractive and had a beautiful personality. After recovering from a broken engagement, I was not quite ready for a new relationship. This young woman was very serious about her worship and service to God. I believed in my heart that she would help me on a spiritual level. Her name was Julie.

Julie was serious about having a relationship. She was not about playing games. I offered her a ride home after church one Sunday afternoon. After that ride home, we began talking regularly. We attended youth services at the church and enjoyed Sunday evening services together. The first time we went out on a date was interesting. Since I did not have a lot of money, we went to Wendy's and I bought an order of small fries which was all I could afford. Luckily she was not hungry! It seemed as if we had known each other for years. Instantly, I felt deep down inside that she was someone I could fall in love with and share my life.

There were many performances that I participated in so I invited her to hear me play. For awhile, I wondered if she would come. Then during one of my solo performances, I happened to look out in the audience. When I saw her, a wave of emotion came over me. Although I was playing Norwegian Woods, my mind was on the prettiest brown-skinned lady in the room sitting on the third row. That was Julie. I played like never before. I knew she had me then!

Julie and I began to spend a lot of time together going to church, concerts and other musical functions. After spending so much time together we fell in love. When we first met, I knew Julie was something special. I quickly came to learn that she was compassionate, loyal and caring with a great sense of humor and she became my best friend. We dated for four years, and on December 25, 1990 we became engaged.

Wedding Vows. In January of 1991 we were married at the Church of God of Prophecy in Lanham, Maryland. We had a small intimate wedding with only a few family members and friends. We laughed because I had only four or five people on my side of the church.

My new wife continued to support me in my music by traveling to different places. Playing my music in different places became a challenge to me because I was not a single man anymore. I had to divide my time wisely because I now had a loving wife in my life.

When I had to practice my saxophone at home the sound was very loud, so my wife had to adjust. When asked to minister at different places, I would have to make sure that my wife was taken care of before I went on these trips. Now that I was married, I had to fulfill my marriage obligations. In Genesis it says "For this cause shall a man leave his father and mother and cleave to his wife and they two shall be one flesh." I was careful not to prioritize my music over her. I still had to do God's will because the talent was given by him, therefore he had to be glorified not matter what the situation or circumstances might have been. I continued to minister at church functions and other religious functions, but not on a large scale.

To me, marriage is one of the God-ordained means for our growth in godliness. It is ultimately about our holiness, not our happiness but I must say, marriage to Julie has made me very happy. She was given to me by God as a gift. When God created both of us, He knew what the other would need.

We were eventually blessed with a baby daughter and what a surprise to me. There I was, thinking I could never be happier since getting married to the lady of my dreams! Well, I acknowledge that the first time I saw our baby daughter, Jyrah, it was at first, a moment of relief, then amazement, and yes, a little shock, too. Being new at fatherhood sparked a little fear of the unknown—there was nothing about growing up with my sisters and learning about women to prepare for this beautiful little baby. If I felt one emotion, I felt them all at the same time. Most of all, I felt proud and thankful to the Lord that she was perfect and safe in Him. I will never forget how soft and cuddly she felt when I held her. I still remember her smell. From the moment I held her, I was captivated and the sense of closeness and gentleness stayed in my head wherever I went. Even though I cannot describe the scent, there was something about it that always relaxed me. It got to a point that anytime I felt stressed, I could simply think about Jyrah. Even today, I can recall that special baby scent sometimes and it gives me such a happy, relaxed feeling. We sat her at the piano on a padded stool before she was 3-years old and turned her on to music appreciation at early age. She would listen for hours during my saxophone practice sessions and was always with us at church.

One day she said to me, "Daddy, I don't want to play the keyboard anymore. I want to play the saxophone."

So when she was at the tender age of 8 years old, we purchased an alto saxophone for Jy. It seemed almost a natural fit for her to play the saxophone so we outfitted her with one as quickly as possible. Wherever we went, she carried hers in a soft case and now Jyrah is an accomplished saxophonist. We have played many duets together. Julie and I are very proud of her. The Lord has been good to my family.

While I am proud that Jyrah has grown into quite a sophisticated, confident young lady who is away at University with plans to study law, there are days when I long for the little sweet baby girl who used to look up at me with those big brown eyes, depending on me for everything. What a gift!

Parents Edwin & Eurina Scatliffe COGOP General Assembly Tabernacle, Cleveland, TN 1989

The Gospel Tones - St. Croix, USVI Youth Convention 1976

Ira with parents

Gospel Tones marching in COGOP parade, St. Croix USVI Youth Convention 1976

Ira cruising with parents' 1976 Cutlass Supreme at Location College USVI 1977

Ira leaving 1973 Ford Pinto Wagon USVI Heading for NYC

Inspirational time of marching around at No. 20 Gamble Gade

No. 20 Gamble Gade

No. 20 Gamble Gade

Parents, Niece, Bro. Gumbo and Daughter waits for Ira

Ira in Jam session Sunday afternoon after church

Ira outside No. 20 Gamble Gade Location (Savan) 1974

Ira playing in Musician's Corner at No. 20 Gamble Gade with Cousin Verdell Turnbull (Bass), Brother Ulric Scatliffe (Guitar), Russell Jones (Keyboard), Ira (Saxophone)

Fellowship at No. 20 Gamble Gade

Ira Ministers on Saxophone for Wash DC National Guard troops

COGOP children singing at No. 20 Gamble Gade 1970's

Ira and Julie's 13th year wedding anniversary

IRA and Julie's engagement party December 1990

Ira and Julie - Wedding Day COGOP, Lanham MD - January 4, 1991

Ira and Julie hanging out after Church Wash, DC 1987

Ira's 1975 Dodge Dart (Ira and Julie's Cruising Classic)

Ira and Julie with Jyrah Lynn at 3 months old

Jyrah's dedication 1995 COGOP Lanham, Maryland

Family portrait Ira, Julie and Jyrah 1996

Jyrah pulling Ira's Saxophone case December 1995

Dadand Jyrah singing March 1996

Jyrah - Playing the Saxophone at age 10

Dad and Jy enjoying a moment

Ira and Julie at Cleveland, TN COGOP General Assembly 1990

Ira and baby Jyrah vacationing at Magens Bay St. Thomas USV

Ira playing America the Beautiful in Woodstock, MD for Correctional Academy Graduating Class 1992

Ordained a Deacon - New Beginnings Church of God of Prophecy September 2011

Anniversary

Ira and Julie New Beginnings COGOP, Lanham MD

Special Anniversary

On the road from St Thomas AP

Aerial View1 of West Indian Dock St Thomas

Aerial View of SubBase

Aerial View2 of West Indian Dock St Thomas

Ira and Julie1 Skyline Dr St Thomas 2007

Ira and Julie2 Skyline Dr St Thomas 200

Magens Bay 2

Memories of St Thomas

Ira and Julie Vacationing in Megans Bay Overloo

Magens Bay 1 from Drakes Seat

Ira and Julie - Jyra Guest Artist

2016 Annual Sisterhood Celebration with Daughter Jyrah

Easter Sunday New Beginnings COGOP 2013

Ira plays at Kathy McGuiness Lt Gov 2016 Campaign event

Ira plays with Jyrah at Kathy McGuiness Lt Gov 2016 Campaign event

Ira following Homegoing for the Egon Matriarch

Ira, Julie, Jyrah at Kathy McGuiness Lt Gov 2016 Campaign event

Jyrah

Ira, Julie, Jyrah join others at Kathy McGuiness Lt Gov 2016 Campaign event

Homegoing Celebration for Egons Mom where Ira was Guest Artis

Chapter 5
Acknowledging Great Men Who Trusted God

I will trust and not be afraid.
Music Corner, No. 20 Gamble Gade COGOP

Some of my friends have looked at unpleasant memories and said they never thought their lives would turn out the way they did and that if they could do it over, they would do things differently. In my case, I have learned that when things did not work out the way I would have wanted, there was clearly a better and greater plan for my future. The focus has to be taken off doubts and placed on God. As I look back over my life, I realize when I thought I was being rejected, I was actually being redirected toward God. No matter how bleak today may look, change is always on the horizon for those of us who have the faith to believe.

We have read many stories about Biblical men from different walks of life who put radical trust in God and yet they had distinct similarities in their approaches to life and the Lord. Habakkuk learned how to trust God and not be affected by the negative stuff going on around him. For example, in Habakkuk 3:17-19, he says, “”Although the fig tree shall not blossom, neither shall fruit be in the vines; the labour of the olive shall fail, and the fields shall yield no meat; the flock shall be cut off from the fold, and there shall be no herd in the stalls: Yet I will rejoice in the Lord, I will joy in the God of my salvation!”

We need to trust in the Lord for He is our help! The passage goes on to say, “…He will make my feet like hinds’ feet, and he will make me to walk upon mine high places. To the chief singer on my stringed instruments!”

If we are not careful, it is easy to get emotionally sidetracked and pulled away from God. When we’re in a tight spot and problems are raging all around, a sense of uncertainty tries to take over the mind. By focusing on our problems and never looking up, we will fail to experience the peace of

God. Isaiah says, "God will keep in perfect peace all who trust in Him, and all whose thoughts are fixed on Him!" It is God who transforms us through every circumstance that comes our way. In all of life's events, we should strive to see meaning in every challenge and trust that God will bring us out and up into His plan for our lives.

It is fascinating to see what common threads could be found in the lives of these incredible men of the Bible who placed their trust in the Lord. In taking a look at several of them we can learn what they had most in common and it is not simply what a person does; it is rather, the heart of a person and how one lives before God. They all experienced some level of the following:

Suffering. They experienced some level of ridicule, humiliation, personal challenges, persecution, or imprisonment.

Acceptance of inevitability death. These men were willing to stand in the face of the enemy and risk death in order to trust God.

Prayer. They were dedicated men of prayer, talking and walking with God. Some did like Elijah who prepared for prayer in and as a result, fire came down from heaven, people turned to the Lord, the enemy's prophets removed, and rain came down from heaven.

Learned to listen. They received and followed instructions God by faith. Limited / removed distractions in their lives. They did not allow others to prevent them from obeying God. They removed the negative influences out of their lives.

Obedience. Whatever God told them to do, they did it without question and without hesitation or delay.

Sometimes the simplest truths are the most profound. It can be easy to get weighed down in heavy theological issues, esoteric topics and technical grammar; none of which is bad in itself, in fact most of it is necessary.

Abraham – the Father of Nations

Abraham found grace in the eyes of the Lord, through faith alone. God drew him to faith and God counted the faith as righteousness - as right standing with God. Yes, he waited for the Promise for years for his son to be born. Yes, he obeyed God and left his homeland. Yes, he was willing to sacrifice his own son that they waited so long to bring into this world. Yes; he held nothing back from God. Yet the Bible says to the one who works, his wage is not credited as a favor, but as what is due. But to the one who does not work, but believes in Him who justifies the ungodly, his faith is credited as righteousness. Clearly there is a way to be right with God that doesn't depend on behavior. Abraham became right with God by faith alone apart from works. It is really simple. Abraham believed God. Now before we spend any more time on the different aspects of faith and all of the various means or manifestation, we need to allow the realization of that simple truth to settle within us. How was Abraham righteous?

Well, God gave a promise and Abraham believed him. It is that simple. God then took this trust and credited righteousness to him. That means that the righteousness was not his own. It was taken as a credit onto Abraham for simply trusting God. Sometimes we can over complicate things. We simply need to trust and believe God. He already set forth his promise of the Gospel. When we believe what God has said about both us and the Gospel of Jesus Christ, then He credits us as righteous. Some of us want the credit and will boast in our success because of our works. Regardless of what we do, even trusting in God, none of it will work without God's regenerative power in enabling us to believe. It would be absurd to take credit for what God does. Without Him, we are nothing.

Noah – The Flood Survivor

Ungodliness was so rampant during those times that God was sorry that He had made man but he found Noah to be righteous and blameless. Noah walked and fellowshipped with God. Only a righteous person can have such connections with God. Hebrews 11:7 states Noah was justified by faith. Noah's faith manifested itself in his obedience in building the ark. Noah He conformed and lived by God's revealed standards of right and wrong reflecting his right standing with God. Walking with God means having faith or constant trust in God concerning the unseen, even when the things we see seem to contradict what God has said (see Heb. 11:7). Noah had found grace in the eyes of the Lord and he walked with God. Though there had never been anything close to a flood that destroyed everything, Noah believed and acted on God's word by faith. Despite opposition and ridicule, he built his whole life around trusting God apart from any tangible evidence that it would happen. He walked with God – he had to be obedient. He was not hypocritical; he did not live a double life. We are not alone when we have to stand alone, because we enjoy fellowship with God.

David – Man after God's Own Heart

Though young, small and seemingly insignificant, he was a man after God's own heart. David trusted God. Though he worked in the sheep pasture, he sang and praised God all day long. Though he was anointed to be king, he wasn't prideful; he continued to trust God. He sought counsel of the Lord. He acknowledged his sin and repented. He respected God's authority and judgment, refusing to kill the Saul, when opportunity came. He honored God anointing. He used the gift of music that God gave him and danced unabashedly naked in the street, letting the whole world know his trust was in the Lord.

Moses – the Deliverer of Israel

Moses' life is generally broken down into three 40-year periods. The first 40-year part of his life involved living in the court of pharaoh where He was instructed in all the wisdom of the Egyptians, and he became mighty in his words and deeds. As the plight of the Hebrews began to disturb him, so Moses took it upon himself to be the savior of his people. Although God did want to use him as His chosen instrument of salvation to save His people, Moses was hot tempered, acting rashly and impetuously. However, it was by faith that He renounced his royal family choosing to help his Hebrew enslaved family. He trusted God though he was rejected and banished from the land. He tried to do what God wanted done but in his own timing. The second 40-year part of the life of Moses encompassed the period of growing and maturing, learning to be humble before the Lord. He learned the simple life of a shepherd, a husband, and a father as God shaped and molded him into what God wanted for His use. This was a period of time that Moses was waiting on the Lord but He was learning how to shepherd, support and raise a family. God was preparing him. These are not trivial things! While we might long for the "mountain top" experiences with God, 99 percent of our lives are lived in the valley doing the mundane, day-to-day things that make up a life. We need to be living for God "in the valley" before He will enlist us into the battle.

The third 40-year period was Moses' role as deliverer and leader of the Israelites in the redemption of Israel. He had a grave responsibility. He was dependent on God's grace and continually pleaded on behalf of the people. He learned to delegate responsibility to other faithful men. The same hot temper that got Moses into trouble in Egypt also got him into trouble during the wilderness wanderings. At Meribah Moses struck the rock in anger in order to provide water for the people but he didn't give God the glory, nor did he follow God's precise commands. Because of this, God forbade him from entering the Promised Land. Moses' life was one of faith, and we know that without faith it is impossible to please God. Likewise, it is by faith that we, looking forward to heavenly riches, can endure temporal hardships in this lifetime (2 Corinthians 4:17-18).

Joshua – the Leader

Joshua was a man of faith and decisive action. God had commissioned Joshua to lead the Israelites into the Promised Land, even though the inhabitants would not be taken without a fight. Joshua's character, his leadership abilities, his faith and readiness typify how Christians can live a victorious life in Christ through faith. Unlike the other spies that went to survey the land of their future, Joshua did not complain and speak words of fear. He had faith that God would deliver them and give them the land of promise. He was an eyewitness to the awesome power and strength of God as the Egyptian army was swallowed by the Red Sea.

From forty years in the wilderness with Moses, Joshua beheld God's provision of manna and clothes that would never wear out. He saw the earth swallow the disobedient and rivers of water spring forth from a rock. His preparation and training was never about his abilities but rather a focus on God's ability and strength. Though they won the battle with the Amalekites proving Joshua's military skills as a general but it was his servant heart that granted him favor with God and Moses. He was obedient to Moses' command and met the Amalekites on the battlefield but during the battle, Joshua knew that his victory lied within God's power and the steadiness of Moses' hand.

When Moses raised up the staff of God, the Israelites had the upper hand. When he lowered the staff, the Amalekites would gain leverage. Choosing to fight this battle required trust and obedience. Being asked to do battle with Amalek is evidence of Joshua's already proven character.

Courage, servanthood, obedience and faith are qualities that make leaders. Joshua is a great example of a man who did not trust in his own abilities but trusted in God's strength to bring forth victory. When we allow God to take the reins in our lives, our hopeless battles become sure wins.

We could go on and on listing men like Daniel and Joseph from the Old Testament, who trusted God. We could also pull out the list from the New Testament and of course, Jesus Christ would come to mind at the top of the list. We should all kneel down and weep, in thanksgiving to the Lord for His faithfulness. Regardless of men's evil plans for us, God has not forgotten us and He is watching over us. We can trust Him through anything.

Chapter 6
Overcoming Jealousy in the Church

Don't worry about those who talk behind your back,
they're behind you for a reason.
Pravinee Hurbungs

We live in a world today where the enemy is rampant, divisive and conniving in his tactics. If we are not careful we can fall into traps that he has set for God's children. How will he do it? He will attempt to destroy us by infiltrating our thoughts with his and by promoting lies through subtle manipulations. Satan's strategy is to get you to put confidence in his resources. He uses techniques designed to attack and control our hearts and minds. He operates through deception, temptation, and accusation. We have to guard against manipulative spirits and not allow lust of the flesh, lust of the eyes or the pride of life to overtake us. (1 John 2:16) We are living in a dissatisfied generation with some people wanting someone else's talents or influence while they ignore the Great Commission right before their eyes. We must put on the whole armor of God in order to be able to stand against the wiles of the devil. (Ephesians 6:11)

It is disappointing to hear someone say, "I wish God made me different" or "If I just had a better voice" or "If I had the gift that you have, I would be doing something special with it." Older people are sometimes jealous of the younger people. In the Church, musicians often envy other musicians; singers and preachers feel envious of those who are similarly called, equipped and gifted. Casual competition may seem harmless but there is danger in informal and professional rivalry. This is one of the enemy's tricks. When a praise and worship leader, (musician or singer), becomes envious of another person due to their potential or perceived success, either of which is larger than the person's own potential or success, it becomes unhealthy.

The Church is both a divine and human institution: divine because it is the assembly of God's redeemed people, both in the Old Testament and in the New. Jesus said, "Upon this rock I will build my church, and the gates of hell shall not prevail against it." (Matthew 16:18) The Church is also called, "The Body of Christ," especially by Apostle Paul in 1Corinthians 12:27, Ephesians 4:12, etc. But the Church is also composed of human beings at different stages of transformation.

Skilled rivalry drive a wedge between people and it has no place in any Christian ministry. It may be discouraging sometimes to see another ministry or person effortlessly achieve the success we desire but we must not forget that God's house is a place where we attend to go to give God praise and worship. We must keep our eyes on Him.

Scripture says that he calls some to be preachers and teachers for the perfecting of the saints. (Ephesians 6:11) He has blessed some with talents and has given supernatural gifts to individuals as He sees fit. The gifts are given for God to be glorified and through them, souls can be delivered from sin and a life of bondage. Blessings come when talents and gifts are displayed without any form of jealousy. Some gifts may be publicly displayed; others may be chosen for specified occasions and all in different ways.

Becoming jealous against a blessed person will not bring forth productive fruits. But in fact, will produce bitterness and as a result, will demonstrate evilness. Often the attention is so focused on the person and the actual gift, that people take their attention off of God and forget to worship Him. And that is where the problem lies. How can we overcome jealousy in the church? We can do this by simply understanding that our brothers and sisters are not our enemies.

Also we can overcome jealousy in the church by understanding that our talents and gifts come from God and one must feel good about another brother or sister's gifts. Every good gift and every perfect gift is from the Lord *(James 1:17)*. We should be joyful as we see the manifestation of these gifts in the church and encourage everyone.

We must realize that having a foothold in the Word of God will break the back of the enemy to the point where division cannot occur. Jealousy does not come from God; it is an evil spirit from the enemy. Therefore jealousy must not be named among us. God created us in order to give Him honor, praise and worship. When we receive a talent from God, it is with the intention that we should honor and glorify Him. The gift that is given to us is also to be used by us in order to bless God's people and ourselves.

Oftentimes, I think we forget that God's given gifts are simply a reward from God that is handed down to particular people. Every single human that has walked this earth was given a talent. Once we discover what the talent is, those of us who serve the Lord should use it in a way in which the world do not hold governance over so that it will bless others. Every part of our life must witness for God, not only what we may say about our faith.

The most powerful witnessing we can do is by our lives, by our daily conduct. The apostle Paul witnessed not only by his words but by his life.

He warned us against being carnally minded telling us that to be carnally minded is death. The carnal mind is enmity against God for it is not (and cannot be) subject to the law of God. (Roman 8:10) We that serve the Lord have received, not the spirit of the world, but the spirit which is of God; that we might know the things that are freely given to us of God. Which things also we speak, not in the words which man's wisdom teacheth, but which the Holy Ghost teacheth; comparing spiritual things with spiritual. *(I Corinthians 2:12-13)*

Professional rivalry has completely disgusted me. I have seen Christian musicians and singers with thinly painted masks of niceties wishing one another well on the surface, while secretly hoping someone might fail. Sometimes, some musicians have refused to allow others to make use of their amplifiers or have stooped so low as to sabotage the equipment, simply to try to make it tougher for the subsequent individual coming on stage. Why would someone seek to raise themselves up by pushing down their brothers and sisters in Christ?

This destroys unity and the Lord cannot bestow blessing upon such people. We must be humble, encourage and exhort others. We need to promote each other. The Lord has called us to humility and servant hood. This is what brings a transfer of the Holy Spirit into our worship. Jealousy is bad for the soul and is destructive.

Some Christians today consider competition as inherently sinful. Others pursue it unreservedly, as if it had no connection to their walk with God. The reality is that competition is unavoidable regardless of our personalities and dispositions. We are compared in school, either for grades or for scholarships; in sports with regularly competition against other teams and musicians compete for top chair positions in the orchestras; actors and actresses compete for lead roles.

We compete in the workforce for jobs, positions and titles. We hear all the time that competition enhances the performance of all participants, not just the winners but it is imperative that we keep our eyes on the

Lord. Colossians 3:23-24 tells us, "Whatever you do, work heartily, as for the Lord and not for men, knowing that from the Lord you will receive the inheritance as your reward. You are serving the Lord Christ". Our desire should be to do as much as we possibly can with the gifts and skills that God gives us — as faithful stewards. So we ought to perform with excellence for His glory and never with the express purpose of hurting others or to in any way injure their efforts.

Noticing the performance of others relative to our own is usually unavoidable. However we should admire and respect those who are more skilled, experienced or accomplished. By humbly acknowledging their abilities and accomplishments, we can learn from them and, by following their example, become better stewards of our talents. Likewise, we should be gracious and humble to those presently less accomplished. In other words, we should recognize that our talents and successes come from God and look for ways to serve others. We should also remember that to whom much is given, much is required, and that — no matter what we've done — others out there have achieved even more. So it's pointless to measure our worth by our accomplishments.

We all may err on one side or the other: some in laziness or misplaced humility failing to give the best. Though man looks on the outward appearance, God looks at the heart *(1 Samuel 16:7)*. Ultimately, it is our faithfulness that pleases God and puts Him on display. So we should wisely steward our God-given talents and gifts for His glory and the good of others.

Jealousy doesn't help us emotionally or spiritually. No one ever becomes perfect on earth, but surely every true Christian becomes more like Jesus, through the sanctifying work of the Holy Spirit. Jealousy and envy are listed among the works of the flesh in Galatians 5:19-21: "Now the works of the flesh are evident, which are: adultery, fornication, uncleanness, lewdness, idolatry, sorcery, hatred, contentions, jealousies, outbursts of wrath, selfish ambitions..." But for all these vices, the same passage also provides an alternative in Galatians 5:22-26: "But the fruit of the Spirit is love, joy, peace, longsuffering, kindness, goodness, faithfulness, gentleness, self-control. Against such, there is no law. And those who are Christ's have crucified the flesh with its passions and desires.

If we live in the Spirit, let us also walk in the Spirit. Let us not become conceited, provoking and envying each another. If the Bible is so clear about these things, no man, however highly placed in the Church, can invalidate these standards. Anyone who calls himself a child of God or a minister of the gospel cannot claim any Biblical support for jealousy or envy. These works of the flesh rule our lives when we are not content with God's blessings. When people do not seek to know what God has blessed them with, but want to be what others are, jealousy and envy take over. Envy and jealousy among servants of God is a display of spiritual immaturity, and God will call every man to account, especially because such display misleads the members and does not edify the Church. It can bring discord, break the unity, diminish integrity and ultimately destroy the membership.

Envy is dangerous; it can lead to killing. It depends on your relationship with Christ. If Christ is in you, there will be a change; everything about you will be new. Without Christ, all you might be doing is pretense and hypocrisy. Christ is the one who enables a Christian to live up to the standard of His calling. So, it depends on your relationship with Christ. Christ being manifested in you will not allow you to engage in envy or walk in jealousy.

Now, why do we have envy and jealousy in the house of God? It shows that the people in the church are simply human. ENVY and JEALOUSY are two of the most terrible, dreadful diseases ravaging the body of Christ today. They are so rampant that you find them at every level in the Church, including the pastoral staff. These are manifestations of carnality among believers. The reason for the reign of envy and jealousy in the Church is that many Christians no longer live by the dictates of the Holy Spirit and have become carnal. They yield more to the flesh than they do to the Spirit of the living God.

The way forward is to go back to God. The Scripture says: "And if my people who are called by my name become humble and pray, and look for me, and turn away from their evil ways, then I will hear them from heaven. I will forgive their sin and heal their land." *(2 Chronicles 7:14)*. It's high time we kicked the devil and carnality out from our midst, and focus on what the Word of God says. If anyone feels another brother or sister is doing well in any way, you should thank God, support and encourage such a person. Pray to God and work hard if you wish to attain that height too. You could even seek counsel from such a person to know the secrets of his success. This should be done with sincerity of heart. This is surely a better way to go, before God, than envy and jealousy. We should stand out positively in our world today, such that we are seen as light, rather than allow worldliness take over our souls. The Bible says: "In the same way, you should be a light for other people. Live so that they will see the good things you do and praise your Father in heaven." *(Matthew 5:16)* God Himself will reward and restore us when we turn back to him.

It is interesting to observe that many forms of ill-health are attributed to long or intense expressions of jealousy. There seems to be something destructive and uncontrollable in jealousy that knows no law, listens to no reason, and will not be restrained even when the effects are self-destructive. It is, therefore, one of the most powerful of the destructive emotions in animals who have the ability to reason or think.

Jealousy is born of a selfish desire to possess and to keep to oneself that which is loved. A person who is affected by jealousy is constantly throwing the entire psychic and physical system of the human body out of harmony with cosmic rhythm. This alone would be sufficient to produce ill health. The continuation of this emotion leads to many forms of mental reactions, which tend to break down mental stability and integrity. In addition to the effect on the physical body, the mind is weakened in its integrity and resistance. To feel jealousy and express it in any form is sure to start the progress of destruction in the physical and mental body of man. When jealousy begins to manifest in destructive ways, the mind begins to weaken in its rationalism and in its ability to comprehend things in their true light. From this moment on, the jealous person is "possessed of evil spirits" and is in truth controlled by one of the darkest forces of the world of evil.

Real love is gracious and kind, seeking to be harmonious with the universal love of God. It seeks not to possess the object of its love nor to limit and restrict being loved by others, but finds happiness and peace in the knowledge that all enjoy that which is worthy of being loved. Any attempt to restrict love by dominating and limiting it will be sure to destroy it, for love is extensive and ever-increasing. It must be unselfish to remain free of the destructive elements. These great emotions are of two classifications: those, which are harmonious with the cosmic laws, and those that are contrary to them. Until man rises above the one and attains glorification in the other, he cannot be truly happy and approach a spiritual kingdom.

Chapter 7
Ministering Through Gospel Music

There is a sound that comes from gospel music that
doesn't come from anything else.
It is a sound of peace.
It is a sound of, 'I'm going to make it through all of this.'
-Yolanda Adams

Whether you instrumentally play, sing or are an avid listener, every note or lyric of gospel music can raise you up out of the pit and bring you to the rock of salvation. Along with good preaching, it has a way of captivating your heart and taking you to another place. However, performing and being involved in gospel music requires a specific mindset. Having witnessed many renditions, I am convinced that humility, servitude, and commitment to God are essential to getting the sincere message of the gospel across to the listening audience.

According to the USA Today April 14, 2015 edition, first lady Michelle Obama endorsed gospel music at the White House Tuesday, calling it a link to God." In her remarks, she referred to it as what helps connect us to God, to that higher power, saying, "For so many, when times have darkened, when there's struggle, gospel music is that ray of hope and it gives you that strength."

Too often, the crowds are thrilled with the extravagant promotion or of the pomp and circumstance surrounding productions and performances. However, while a lot of music may be exhilarating and entertaining, none of it will be effective for the kingdom of God. The world is full of entertainers who can temporarily take your mind off of the stresses of the day – but they cannot save anyone's life for all eternity. Gospel musicians, artists and singers must seek and stay before God because the purpose of Gospel music is to bring the message of Christ to a lost and dying, sinful world.

Functioning in your calling. We live at a unique time in history where there are vast opportunities for all of us in ministry. Everyone has a very specific and unique high calling – no matter our age, race, gender, upbringing, or background. If we are not doing it today, we should rise up and begin to function in our calling. Even if you think you are already functioning in that calling, I believe it is God's will to take you ever higher. For example, I grew up in the Church and have a music ministry background. This is what I know and enjoy. This is where I thrive and am comfortable. However, God has taken me to a higher level where ministering in gospel music does not stop with a stage performance but rather, it segues into teaching, preaching and leading others.

Every person is born with a predisposition toward independence from God. That disposition tends to harden as the person gets closer to adulthood. If the gift of salvation is received, then God will begin inwardly transforming the person. Our calling is not to entertain but to do what God has purposed for our lives. Mentoring, parenting, and spiritually guiding new believers toward God is a subsequent outreach follow-on necessity. We must determine what our calling from God is and actively work to help and encourage others to grow in Christ.

Whatever the present circumstances and geographical location, God can raise us up, equip, and release us to advance His Kingdom. We are here for such a time as this. *(Esther 4:14)* We should desire to make a difference in our generation. God has already designed a ministry for each of us. Perhaps we get in a rut because we are comfortable where we are, or we are bound by a local ministry or pastor that is unsupportive. Some of us are afraid to make a change or to do something different, but if we will surrender, God will move us forward. He gave some to be apostles, prophets, evangelists, pastors and teachers, to prepare God's people for works of service, so that the body of Christ may be built up). *(Ephesians 4:7-11&12)*

Are you functioning in your calling? Your ministry will come out of your relationship with God – He comes first. He may use your talents and your gifting, but only if you are surrendered to Him because He wants to supernaturally empower you. With all of my 40 years of playing, I cannot accredit any of it to me. Out of my desperation to learn how to play the saxophone, it was God who taught me everything I know and I have yielded my playing to Him.

Though people laughed before I had mastered the saxophone and while I could not break through certain barriers to join the U.S. Coast Guard military band, I have come to rely completely on God. He has affirmed anointed, and called me for such a time as this.

We must refuse to be limited by life's circumstances and move forward in our calling. When we do this, God can bring the release and breakthrough necessary to help us recognize the specific ministry designed for us. It is the only way possible to advance and function according to God's plan or purpose for our lives. Whatever the ministry, we should not be in isolation but must be in unity with and in submission to the body of Christ under God's delegated leadership authority.

Ministering the gospel and functioning in your calling, comes with responsibility. However, as you take your eyes off the enemy and allow God to nurture you, your ministry will grow and develop. We can function full time in our ministry and be successful if we obey God. Character is as important as the ministry and it will be reflected by your obedience. Your success will also be reflected by your obedience. God told us this from the beginning and He has not changed. (Joshua 1:8) Once we learn this most invaluable lesson and allow God to teach us, our perspective on life will change and we will become successful.

Ministering in Gospel Music. Many artists have great talent and are impressive gospel music performers on the stage but if they are not anointed, it will not break people free of their chains. Instead, the crowds will hear it, get excited and dance to the music, then go home only to return to the same manner of living and squalor. If your calling is to minister in gospel music, it is important for you to remember that it is only the anointing that will break the yoke. Therefore, ministering in Gospel music must be different because it is music that is ordained by God to spread the good news. It is the message of Jesus Christ to people everywhere through music and spiritual hymns.

As ministering servants, we must focus on delivering the message and not fall into the trap of performing gospel music to make a living. Very often the enemy attaches himself to the Gospel music business process which eventually leads into a desire for fame or fortune. The music is not effective if it is simply performed or delivered as a technical rendition. It must be done with meaning in order for souls to be blessed through the hearing and urgent proclaiming of the good news of Jesus Christ. Mixing gospel music with the secular world in order to acquire spiritual benefits will only have a counter affect.

Every since I was little, I have heard the famous Abe Lincoln quote, "You can fool all the people some of the time, and some of the people all the time, but you cannot fool all the people all the time."

Sometimes, we also quote a familiar passage from the Bible, "You shall know the truth and the truth shall set you free." More accurately, that verse starts out by stating, "Then said Jesus to those Jews which believed on him, If ye continue in my word, then are ye my disciples indeed; And ye shall know the truth, and the truth shall make you free." *(John 8:31-32)*

This music must be separated from the world or it will be impure and fail to accomplish its purpose. Only the true gospel can set us free. We can mix different liquids or substances with water and still try calling it water. We can even present it that way. However, your system and vital organs know the difference and will regurgitate if something foreign or impure enters whether in disguise or if it is an overt intrusion. Gospel artists today must understand that concept.

Without a foundation in historical church principals, many of today's artists are like a sounding brass or tinkling cymbal. (1 Corinthians 13:1). Unfortunately, they are often completely unaware. How can they minister and deliver the good news of God's love if they have not experienced it? Many of them confuse their human spirit with God's Holy Spirit but they are offering a counterfeit message to the world.

Only the anointing is effective where the jagged edges of life's most persistent problems are weighing people down to destruction. Gospel music under the anointing offers deliverance, freedom, restoration, healing, and renewed. It also brings joy, peace and meditation for your soul.

Musicians at Work in the Church. Worship is an integral part of the Church assembly and we must protect the worship atmosphere. It is the anointing that makes the difference. Gifted musicians are those whom God has anointed to play an instrument in an attitude of worship. While most people are unable to discern the difference between talent and the anointing, the enemy knows. He sets unique decoys particularly designed to trap musicians. Anointed musicians are usually talented, but not all talented musicians are anointed. Talented individuals who serve in positions reserved for individuals anointed by God, are often unable to sustain their character. Just being able to play an instrument does not qualify anyone to bring others into the presence of the Lord or even be part of a worship team.

The enemy has a way of finding the right button to push in order to bring unrest and discord in order to disturb a musician's peace. Since a musician's talent is usually measured by acclaim, we are especially subject to the desire for fame, achievement or acceptance. We must guard against the temptation to steal God's glory, especially in worship. Musicians at work in the church must understand the criticality of worship and encourage authenticity. Only true worship will have an impact on God's own children.

Voluntary or Compensation. I have one simple question: What is it about musicians that makes the Church question whether to pay them? Is it because musicians seem to enjoy what they do? Is it possible that what they do seems effortless for them to render music and sing songs? Why is it that those who disagree with paying musicians seem to be so angered by the discussion? Some people think that paying the musicians pollutes the ministry.

Music is a ministry but some churches believe that because of that fact, it must be done with volunteers. In some instances, there may be an available person who will play the piano or direct the choir. If possible to get volunteers to offer their time and talents to the work of ministry in the church, it can be good – but not always. Some churches are able to pay staff selectively but not everyone, so it is up to the ministry. Some volunteers may invest as much time as the musicians so the question comes up – why pay the musicians?

Other churches maintain a particular standard of music and may be willing to offer a salary commensurate with maintaining the repertoire of vocal, choral and organ music. The music budget and endowments may be established to help with the funding. These people understand the scripture about the workman being worthy of his hire and that its application is not limited to the preaching pastor. We all understand that when a person is paid, the church has a right to expect a higher level of commitment.

It is interesting however, that we do not seem to battle the question of the validity of compensation pertaining to anyone else – but we go up-in-arms if we suggest having to pay someone to play a piano or strum a guitar. This is fascinating but it is also ignorant. There has been considerable selfishness, inconsideration and lack of respect toward these selfless individuals.

Volunteering is precisely that. However, there are pros and cons to both sides. The joy of volunteering is that it usually involves fewer hours, flexibility, more about personal passions, a laid back attitude, and personal fulfillment. The downside to it is the management of it is often a bit disorganized with a lack of direction and lack of continuity – the flow can be off-track. With paid musicians, compensation does create a greater sense of obligation so there is definitely a different feeling. However, with it come planning, management, organization, program continuity and synchronization, greater expectations from the church and a level of commitment that offers some assurance for the different services. Also, the music is more likely to be of a certain quality because of the set expectations.

We have taken our musicians for granted for years and when they "burnout" and seek employment using their talents, they are criticized, tossed aside and even condemned to hell. We want them but only on our terms.

No wonder so many have left the Church. We have complained about them leaving but have done little to encourage them to stay. We essentially treat them as if they are the average church member sitting on the pew. Well, I have news for you – they are not average. They are those who have been chosen, anointed and appointed to minister to the church. Yet we charge them with treason if they seek compensation or if they elect to go anywhere else.

Musicians usually do not want to leave the place where they feel a connection with the ministry; they usually leave under duress – but only as a last resort. They are often scrutinized and castigated by people whose only sacrifice is to rise up and come to worship service. Those who are in demand spend many hours during the week in agony of preparation. They love what they do, and they want to do it well. It requires hours of practice and the dedicated ones will give everything they have to make sure the service is a tremendous blessing to God and His people, sometimes to the point of exhausting themselves. Those who are anointed by God do not want to disappoint the ministry – ever. They will do everything possible to ensure the music goes on in the event they cannot attend a particular service. However, they often pay a great personal price. They alone, are responsible for expenses associated with their professional equipment, training and education, tools, peripheral devices and any secondary services required to maintain their provision of service. Worshipping musicians are on the front line of the battle! When they come forth during worship service, they are expected to minister to the people despite the attacks of the enemy and their personal challenges. The added pressure that comes with the responsibility and commitment to the Church is overwhelming. It is unfathomable that ungrateful members and leaders would treat outsiders better than they would the very ones who lift up praises to God and helps usher the people into worship.

The musicians make themselves available despite their own heavy load. Many are just happy to use their instruments for the Lord. But make no mistake – just by the nature of being musicians, these people suffer for the body of Christ. Their sacrifice is not small in God's eyes. He sees them in their personal struggles.

If the Church has mistreated people or has not paid them as worthy of their hire, it is a disgrace and dishonor to the name of Jesus. They are worthy of their hire. Anyone of decision making authority or sitting in positions of power who is compensated for service in the church but refuses to consider properly honoring those in specialized service, whether musicians or otherwise, is a thief and a liar. Leadership will be held accountable. The reference is with respect and appreciation for the local ministry, its congregation, the ministry platform, the demands upon the talent and gifts in the ministry, the capacity for volunteers and the impact of the music program, and extent of the Church's ability to sustain a music department. Regardless, if the Music department is a full time ministry with a demand for specialized talents, the Church administrators are responsible for developd the Music Department should collaborate to come up with a plan that ensures the budget is allocated and expended appropriately. Musicians need to be able to eat and feed their families just as others do. Or course some are purely voluntary and not in position to command a fee. However, those who are on staff, expected to be in place and in attendance at key functions, or those whose impact greatly affects the ministry should be considered essential to the church and therefore adequately compensated.

Personally, I have heard all kinds of excuses from church people and am amazed at how sanctimonious people can be about some things but not about other, more important administration decisions. For example, may God bless those who can give their services free, but a man is also worthy of his hire.

Churches today preach about giving as much money and time to the church as possible. That is not what Paul teaches in 2 Corinthians. "Each man should give what he has determined in his own heart to give, for the Lord loves cheerful giver" – Not a guilt driven one!

My comment to the Church is short and simple. You can see them in the section under Straight Talk at the end of this book.

Chapter 8
Taking Your Gift Seriously

No two people on earth are alike, and it's got to be that way in music or it isn't music.

- Billie Holiday

The Bible speaks about gifts and talents. Having God's gifts is not meant for us to get the glory so we must not take this gift lightly. We also have to be careful how it is used. Having a bad attitude, arrogance and all the negative things that human perform will not transpire into blessings. One thing that we must keep in mind is staying humble, no matter how great your accomplishments or no matter how good you are at what you do. The talent did not come from us but from God.

We must be aware of the tactics that the enemy uses to distract us and to get us off point. Having a God-given talent must be used properly. When it is not used properly, it could be taken away from us.

God bestows gifts upon members of the body of Christ which are intended to be used for the common good of the church and of humanity. For example, gifts endowed by the Spirit for functions are recognized by the church in pastoral, evangelistic, apostolic, and teaching ministries particularly needed to equip the members for service, to build up the church to spiritual maturity, and to foster unity of the faith and knowledge of God.

However, Peter also said that "each has received a gift" *(1 Peter 4:10)* and our gifts are not an accident of genetics and experience. God knew what he was doing when he made each of us and has intentionally given us the gifts we have in the measure we need. Therefore, we are to be good stewards of the gifts God has entrusted to us. He has entrusted them to us primarily for the benefit of others (1 Peter 4:10; Romans 12:4–6). Our gifts are not intended to be platforms where we try to gain our sense of significance from the esteem of men. Our real significance comes from God who chose us in Christ. He gifted and sent us forth in the kingdom of God for His purposes. There is more significance there than we can fully comprehend and appreciate. The praise of men is can be dangerous. We must take a serious look at ourselves and see how praise affects us. Some of us are lifted up by it but we should be humbled by it. A man is tried by his praise. *(Proverbs 27:21)*

Sometimes, musicians have a tendency to forget the purpose for which they were gifted. Instead of allowing the praise to go to God, they keep it for themselves. Jesus said, "If I glorify myself, my glory is nothing." *(John 8:24)* This word strikes deep. It cuts through all self-praise, all pleasure in praise, and taking home to our hearts what others say of us. We must be careful about receiving praise. Spiritual flattery sounds good, but the best place for praise is at the foot of the Cross. This is different from encouraging words spoken to us or compliments we receive.

Let us be reminded to keep Jesus at the center of our hearts. All praise belongs to the Lord. I am thinking of that deadly thing of the praise of man that brings a snare and not a blessing. Jesus refused it when Satan tried to tempt Him in the wilderness. Look how powerful His ministry was. Imagine if He had fallen for the tricks of the enemy. Some of the most talented people in the world who started out in the Church singing gospel were tempted at young ages to leave the choir in search of fame or fortune. Many of them were even encouraged by their own parents who thought it was a way to make a little extra cash or to help pay the bills. It starts out so innocently enough, but before long, it wrecks the soul. Our Lord utterly refused it, ignored it, and turned from the temptation.

We are on assignment from God. As servants of the Lord we must be good stewards of the gifts we have received. Others need the benefits of our gifts. That's why we have them. We are not our own. *(1 Corinthians 6:19)* Our lives are not about pursuing our dreams. Many of our dreams stem from pride and are self-exalting. If we were to take a magnifying glass or put our hearts under a microscopic lens, we might discover that most of us are gratuitously selfish when we really examine our motive.

God knows what He made us for and where we should be positioned. He places us where we can sacrifice and give of ourselves to the fullest and be most fruitful. By faith, He will lead us in the most ultimately fulfilling paths even when those paths lead through suffering and death.

By aspiring to be fruitful and the very best for God's glory, we can live out our assignment for the sake of others. We must not dishonor God by devaluing the gifts he's given us. In other words, don't waste valuable time grumbling about gifts you don't have or resenting others for the gifts they do have. *(Matthew 25:14-29)* The Bible also teaches us to not neglect the Gift that is within us. We need to take heed to what God has called us to do. That which we have received from the Lord we must use it to fulfill the calling upon our lives. *(1 Timothy 4:14).*

We are accountable for the gifts that the Lord has given up and therefore should use them to honor God for the good of the people in the interest of the Lord. When we devalue our gifts, it is equivalent to declaring that the Lord is a hard man, as if He does not know what He is doing. Such a person has not really known the Lord because if he had, he would have true affection for and faith in the Lord. That person would not question God's decision to give gifts to anyone and would not judge the assignments that He made. The Lord is wonderful. The gifts of the Lord will also keep you strong and draw you close to His presence.

We must not complain even if others are sinfully prideful. Just pray for them when they stumble. God knows how to oppose them *(1 Peter 5:5).* There is no higher calling for you than to be you, and God will reward you beyond your wildest dreams if you faithfully steward your gifts for others.

Personal faith will help during the tough times and keep one centered and grounded. When we take our gifts seriously, we must steward the whole package. This includes taking care our health and body. Staying in God's presence and under the anointing will ensure that we are in tune with the congregation and music program. We must learn how to work with the minister, the staff, the congregation, and support the different choirs and ensembles. If you are a musician, you must be a "people person." There is no way around that because you cannot minister to people if you don't like them or want to be near them. We should never be satisfied to stay where we are but should always practice. Equally as important, we must stay relevant to the times. This means we should keep moving, learning, and growing.

The most important requirement for a church musician is the ability to see the big picture and to respond to it effectively.

Many congregations have had their melodic senses dulled by too much overpowering instruments. People need to hear their own voices, and they need to be needed as part of the service. If the instruments never stop playing, people will drop out and no one will notice. Let the congregation become acquainted with their own sound, especially if this is in their own service. Above all, play your instrument toward heaven. Focus on God in every part of the selection. If your goal is to please Him more than yourself or anyone else, then you will bless His people. Your heart should be offered to God continually and not struck in awe or carried away by the sound of your instrument. Your gift comes from the Lord.

Chapter 9
Enduring Through Trials and Tribulations

Courage is what it takes to stand up and speak;
courage is also what it takes to sit down and listen.
Winston Churchill

I spent six months on what was referred to as the 2-10 shift. This was a challenging time for me and my family. The trials and tribulations were rough. My wife had to undergo a major operation after she became ill. It was terribly devastating for me to have to leave my wife and daughter at home by themselves. The sadness and hurt went deeper than I could have ever imagined. The amazing thing though, was how easy it was for me during this time to witness and tell other people about God's goodness. There was something almost supernaturally therapeutic at work through this part of my journey. It was a period of testing and this was the time I would see if all I believed was going to transpire in my life.

During these seriously challenging times, the enemy tried to persuade me to turn back from the Lord. He wanted me to doubt God and did everything possible. He knew I was in the heat of the moment, and that the intensity of the fiery trials I faced were turned up hotter like the fire of the pit used to destroy the three Hebrew boys, Shadrach, Meshach and Abednego. However, they stood firmly on that sure foundation and challenged King Nebuchadnezzar when faced with the decision of worshipping a pagan idol.

Maybe the enemy thought that I would turn my back on God. The Scripture states: "Acknowledge him in all thy ways and he will direct your path." Keeping this scripture close to my heart and in mind all day long while praying and believing, building up my strong faith and having a made up mind, I walked the floors. The prayers of my brothers and sisters in the Lord in the heavenly spiritual realm kept me going and I continued to play my saxophone without missing a beat.

I was transferred back to the 10-6 shift and remained assigned to this unit. Then in December 2009 I was involuntarily transferred to the Jessup Correctional Institute, in Jessup, Maryland. I did not like all of these changes and became furious about what was happening with my job. I was assigned to the 11-7 shift. I only knew a few people at this institution. Everything was new for me. The security level was higher and the environment was more dangerous. I left home late and returned home even later. This was a challenging time for me mentally, physically and spiritually. It was as though there was an assault on my very being and the only way I would be able to survive this was to stay focused on and glorify God. I had to believe the Lord – I knew that if I lost faith, it would be the end of me and I could not do that. My family needed me and I needed them. It came to a point where I constantly evaluated and challenged myself, wondering if I was going to pass this test or curious as to whether it was even possible to pass the test.

Once I settled down at the new institution, I whispered quietly to the Lord, "God, I know you are with me." After a few months I gradually accepted my new circumstances, but still did not understand my calling was to play the saxophone.

Prior to being transferred to the new Institution I attended A Manpower Conference in Washington, D.C. hosted by Bishop T.D. Jakes, Senior Pastor of the Potters House in Dallas, Texas. God revealed many different things to me. The music was uplifting and the message preached on the last day of the conference brought tears to my eyes. Bishop Jakes was preaching about stirring up the gift in you. It was all I could do to hold up my head, I was a bucket of water. It was perfect timing on the job - I had the weekend off and I really needed to be at this conference. It worked out for me. God knows exactly what we need, all we have to do is trust him.

After giving a small offering at the conference, I took the Washington, D.C. metro transit home with only enough money left for the fare. I found myself crying like a baby and hoped I didn't run into anybody that I knew. I didn't want anyone to see me crying like this. I was touched by the message and how the Holy Spirit was dealing with me. God is amazing!

When I got home I heard music playing. I realized that the music was coming from my stereo, which my wife was playing. It was unusual for her to be playing music on my stereo. The song being played was "Stir up the Gift" by the Colorado Mass Choir. This was a sure confirmation from God. This made me cry even harder.

My wife asked me, "Did someone mess with you"?

"No," I replied. I told her that this is the Spirit of God moving inside of me and the power in the message from Bishop Jakes.

As I thought about my financial hardships it was then that I realized that one day I would be a millionaire and my music would be successful and great things would happen to me and my family spiritually.

For awhile I took a breather and began to think back on my life. It was something I began doing a lot lately. Sometimes, we do not understand where God is leading us but He will hold us and guide us along the way and then one day it will all come together. Even though it may look as though we are living beneath our privilege sometimes, or as if our lives are not where we want them, but God's timing is so perfect. I could think back on the people I grew up with and see where God has brought me from and how He has kept me all of these years.

Fondest memories. Some of my best days were in the days of Bishop Amos Carty, Sr. especially when he was overseer of the Leeward Islands. He served several terms there. The first was between 1978-1982 and then again from 1994-1999. It was during the first period that I have such fond memories. I loved Bishop Carty. He was a busy man, quite knowledgeable, well versed, cultured and well traveled and most importantly, he had a really nice car. When Bishop Carty would depart St. Thomas and head over to the Leeward Islands, he would ask me to take care of the family while he was away. So since no one else in the family had driving skills, it was my job to provide transportation for the children to and from private school and help his wife with errands. This often meant I was able to keep the beautiful Chrysler Cordova in my care for several weeks at a time. On the days when I could not get the family car from my parents, they got no back talk from me. "No problem," I would say. "I am sure I will be able to think of something!"

Of course, I was secretly planning to use the fancy Cordova. I enjoyed those days, especially when the girls were giving me those long side glances!

As a child growing up in the 70's, it was challenging because in that era everything was about church. Coming from a Christian home, we had to go to Sunday School -- we had no choice. Then there was vacation Bible school. It was great fun and beyond learning about the Bible, there was Sister Ruby.

Sister Ruby Vanterpool. If ever there was a gift from God, it was Sister Ruby. There are a lot of sisters in the world, but very few Sister Ruby's. This particular Sister practically ran vacation Bible school where she kept the children in order and gave us godly instructions. Her wisdom has greatly influenced my life. She taught us the books of the Bible, children's choir songs and how to be respectful. When she finished with me, I could list and describe all of the key Biblical characters. We were not scared of her but did not think of disrespecting her. She kept us in check at times when our parents could not do it and she did not make excuses for our behavior. I am a grown man and still call her Sister Ruby to this day and I still have the utmost respect for her. Thank God for pioneers like Sister Ruby Vanterpool.

Growing up as a child and spending my teenage years attending the Church of God of Prophecy at No. 20 Gamble Gade was a fun time for me. There was a lot of character in the old church. There was no shortage of that. We had some older members at that time, who were very funny and when they testified, they explained everything in detail. They made us laugh as they unreservedly acted out their testimonies. Sometimes, we would be embarrassed because of the things they said or did as they painted a picture of their situation and how they overcame their challenges. If some of those testimonies had to be rated, my guess it their stories would be banned. Overall, however, they were very serious about their faith in God and personally speaking, I wish we had more transparency these days. Today everybody is too sophisticated. I miss the days when people were dependent upon God and not too prideful to publicly testify about how He turned around a situation their lives. Yes, testimony time in the old days was real good.

Sister Inez. Then there was Sister Inez in the USVI. If the band did not play the song, "Be Ready When the Bridegroom Comes" exactly right, she would come over to where we were and make all kinds of faces and motions with her hands to let us know how she felt. Some of us used to duck down but if we were still playing, that was not so easy. She would make some real strange gestures. We didn't know for sure if she was working something for us or against us – we just knew we better get that musical note right the next time around or Sis. Inez would be coming for us.

Jamaican brother. In New York, we had a brother from Jamaica who testified of how he went to do a job for lady but she did not have the money to pay him but she would offer an alternative in exchange for his services. Instead of fixing it up and saying something like, I was faced with a compromising situation or temptation but God delivered me, this brother stood up in church and said, she wanted to give him – well, "sex". Of course, he recounted the entire exchange; it was very colorful to say the least, without cleaning up the story. Although I was pretty young, I knew those sidelong glances that were exchanged between my mother and some of the other women, meant this was taboo. At the same time, some of the men were doing their best to hold back the laughter. When I saw tears streaming down one of my sister's faces (and she was always straight-faced and serious in the church), that's when I knew I really loved this church. I was never going to leave there. Everybody was free to give their testimony, no matter how colorful the story was. If we could have fast forwarded to today's living, we probably could have started a reality show. We had enough material just from one testimony service!

Faithfulness. People didn't get sick and messed up with strange disease and cancer because they were not harboring unforgiveness in their hearts nor were they stressing themselves by holding back on their true feelings. If something was wrong, you spoke it out, we prayed about it and moved on.

Natalie Jones. There was a great love for the Church back then. Even though none of us was famous, we had our own local fan club. You don't see that as much in the church today. However, we were fortunate to have someone like Natalie Jones who went everywhere with us, taking pictures and journaling or documenting our performances. It was the outward unabashed enthusiasm of the members that kept our musicians and the Music Department alive.

Chapter 10
Trusting God

Without having money or seeing a way out.
Faith is taking the first step, even when you don't see the whole staircase.
Martin Luther King, Jr.

Julie and I had been married for about 3 months and I was challenged again, but in a different way. It occurred to me recently, that doing a lot, ministering through music, you discover that the more you do, the less money you have. Yet, God will make a way out of the commitments you have.

For a short period of time, I worked at a music store in Rockville, Maryland where I cleaned and performed minor repairs on woodwind instruments. Being around musical instruments was good for me so I thought this was the one job after all of these years, that I would truly enjoy. The money I earned was not economically sufficient but working in a music store and being around all of that sophisticated equipment and latest technology made me feel like I was alright.

When an opportunity came about for me to attend a Chaplain and Chaplain's Assistant Conference in Indiantown Gap, Pennsylvania in March of 1991, the thought was rather irresistible. After all, having grown up in the Church, this was something I felt would be easy for me since I was very experienced and well versed in the principles of prayer.

This particular conference was specifically designed and tailored for the Army and National Guard reserves forces. While getting ready for a session, I was taking a shower one day when one of the conference soldiers who was also in the shower area, began asking me questions about the type position or job I currently held in the National Guard.

Very quickly, the enemy whispered some negative thoughts and said, "Why is he talking to you in the shower? He is gay; do not talk to him."

However, something else deep down on the inside of me said, "You'd better listen to him."

Outwardly, my response to the man was, "I do not have a real job right now – only the National Guard Reserves and of course, that is only temporary assignments." This involved serving with the D.C Metropolitan police department, the U.S. Customs conducting some drug interdiction work which was a continuum of events focused on interrupting illegal drugs smuggled by air, sea, or land and normally consisted of several phases – cueing, detection, sorting, monitoring, interception, handover, disruption, endgame, and apprehension – some which may occur simultaneously.

So given that this was only a temporary assignment and I was looking for a long-term, permanent opportunity that would pay well and allow my career to grow, I decided to listen to the man. God often has blessings for us, but unwittingly, we allow the enemy to trick us out of His blessings. In retrospect, I could see that had I listened to the enemy I would have missed out on the very opportunity that I was seeking. The soldier said, "I am a state of Maryland Correctional Officer. Would you like to become a state Correctional Officer?"

This was a point in my life that I really needed good, stable but meaningful employment. I had helped people and had been looking for God to bless me, but I was still not where I felt I should be and was not functioning in my calling. Maybe this would be that opportunity so I replied, "At this point in my life it does not matter what type of work I do; I just need full time employment."

Once the seminar was over, I received the packet of information on how to become a correctional officer. After returning home, I took the advice from the soldier after giving it plenty of thought. Since I trusted and believed that God would give me a job, I decided to apply for the position of correctional officer. Everything was working according to God's plan toward placement for the job. For example, I passed the written examination, the background checks, and the physical examination – all with not one problem – and got accepted for the job within a short period of time. The academy, which was a 6-week period of training, was located in Woodstock, Maryland.

My academy training completed in September of 1992, and I was chosen as the graduating class commencement speaker! How amazing is that? Apart from words of thanksgiving and praise, I don't remember a word I said that day. All I could think of was that the Lord had showcased my talent for the graduating class. He raised me up in order for me to play my saxophone. This was a perfect way to conclude the training. I performed the rendition of America the Beautiful. I can almost tell you where everybody was standing and I can almost remember the expression on my family and everybody else's face. It was a high celebration for me personally because I could now freely play my saxophone in front of the prison officials with my head held high. I was finally vindicated; I was no longer rejected; and I was, at long last, free to lift up my horn publically in praise to God for all to see.

The new correctional Officers and staff received the song very well. Within days, I was assigned to the Jessup Correctional Institution, in Jessup Maryland and was directed to work on the 10-6 shift, also known as the midnight shift. I continued to minister in music at church functions and other religious activities. Though many people complained about it, the midnight shift was a blessing to me because it gave me the opportunity to attend Sunday morning church services.

Occasionally if I had to minister on the weekend, I would minister and still have time to report to work on time, because a great deal of my engagements were performed before 9:00 pm. I could minister and still be at work by 10: 00 pm.

Through all of the assignments, I still praised God. No matter what came my way, I still praised God. I believe I am alive today because I still praise God!

Conclusion

"These are the times that try men's souls."

Thomas Paine, The American Crisis

Even though this book encapsulates much of my philosophy on using our talents and gifts in the Church and the importance of knowing our worth and value, there is another side of my personality that I want to share with you.

The Virgin Islands was a fabulous place to grow up. I spent early years attending a primary school and received my secondary education at the best school in St. Thomas where I intermingled with students from different backgrounds. What impressed me most was how my school's education was geared toward nurturing and preparing me for a life of service and leadership. Most children walked to school; I drove mom and dad's car. Most kids played softball; I played saxophone. Other boys had a dog for a pet; I had a dog and a chicken. Other kids were worried about how they looked and what people thought about them. I was more concerned about how I made people feel when I played on my saxophone.

Life was good in those days but looking back in life's mirror, a great many lessons have been learned.

While I was growing up in school, I was also growing up in Church. My church education prepared and guided me for a life of spiritual service, warfare and the frontline in ministry. The Bible provides us with many examples of how to prepare for war. Fasting and praying always signified the building and strengthening of our faith. The praise would always go out first, for praise is the forerunner to victory.

It was praise that I felt drawn to in ministry and I was always determined to be the best at everything I did. It was a mark of excellence in my family. Therefore, I constantly worked at enhancing my music abilities and tried to prove myself worthy to people. I especially sought validation and approval of those people who did not think I would make it as a musician. After all of my years of playing saxophone, my peace really came when I realized that happiness does not come from how others look at you; it comes from how you look at others. My life in Christ changed everything because my view of others had everything to do with His view of me. The King of Kings accepted me; He accepted my praise. We can never be happy with more until we are first happy with what we currently have. It was as though God planted a seed of desire within me to please Him. He has truly rewarded my life with more than I could ever have imagined. What He gave to me years ago is now reflected in the outward manifestation of these talents and gifts today.

Many times in the early days of my playing, I masked my feelings to avoid letting others know that I was deeply hurt and discouraged. With a little help from my sense of humor and other playful aspects of my personality, I managed to hide my feelings. As I think back on it, I did a really good job of holding onto rejection and the pain of my talents and gifts not being received or promoted in my youth. Learning to let go while at a young age was difficult, but I have learned that lesson. Sometimes it's just better to let things go. As life progressed, I stopped holding onto disappointments and let go of the pain. Eventually, I managed to swap out childhood grudges for adult biblical principles that teach us how to freely forgive others. When I learned how to let things go and how to forgive others, I became truly satisfied and a happy person. In fact, the bigger the wrong I forgave, the better I felt.

Some of the people who put me down in the early years of my playing have led disappointing lives. My heart actually goes out to them because there, but by the grace of God, goes I.

Even though I have been treated badly many times by well meaning people, mishandled by the Church, and stuck in tight places by good intentioned "saints of God" which tempted me to be a bit skeptical, the realization that all of us, even the people who treated me poorly, are still in God's hands, has kept me humble. Not one of us is perfect. Some of the very musicians that everyone thought were most likely to succeed in music are no longer on the circuit. Many of them are not playing musical instruments anywhere publicly. Things change and we are constantly surprised by the twists and turns in life.

While I still work to continue improving, it is no longer to prove myself to others. I have learned to stay true to God and to myself.

Eleanor Roosevelt said, "No one can make you feel inferior without your consent."

Everything about the small stuff is just that – so we must not sweat the small stuff. Instead, I have learned to live life with a passion for what God cares about in this life. He loves people and so do I. Jesus was mishandled, mistreated and misrepresented but He didn't say a word.

He did not rush to promote Himself; neither did He make anyone feel like less of a person for all they did to Him. Instead He prayed for them. Good things come to those who wait.

Everything changes. Although it is almost impossible to recognize the changes from day-to-day, when we look back ten years from now, it's all different. If I were to sum up my life's experiences, I could do it in three words and it would go like this.

Life is a gift.

Having a sense of belonging to God in a covenantal sense, is what has saved my life. He created me for His purpose.

All those years ago, when I frequently dreamed and made plans about what I was going to do "one day" to make my mother and father proud of me. I had no idea where I would be today. However, I knew I wanted my epitaph to say more than I was born, and died. As far back as the sixth grade, when other kids were goofing off, I was thinking on how my life would count for God. As we know, our children need to be taught who they are in Christ so they can live faithfully.

Paul was in the midst of a tempest. Yet somehow, he had an amazing calm in the midst of this storm. We also have our storms in life, and we wonder how to get through them. Paul had a few "secrets" that helped him to survive life's challenges.

The most important one that he reminded us of was that he belonged to God. Paul said, "Last night an angel of the Lord to whom I belong and whom I serve stood beside me." Belonging to Jesus makes all the difference in your life. Only a follower of Jesus Christ has this confidence. Repeatedly in the Scriptures, we are given the analogy of being in a relationship with God like that of a bride to a husband to whom she is deeply in love. This reminds us of His affection and love toward us. We are also reminded in John 10, that He is "the good Shepherd and we are his sheep." This reminds us of His constant care and awareness of where we are and what we are experiencing. In the analogy of a sheep belonging to a shepherd, it sounds good. However, have you ever thought of what it really means?

Sheep are basically defenseless, vulnerable, and dim-witted. They cannot fend for themselves. However, when the sheep are under the care of a loving shepherd, they are safe and content. Well, I will refrain from referring to myself as dim-witted, but I will say that I have learned to trust in the Lord for everything. I can come to the Lord and bring Him all my cares also, because like Romans 8:15 reminds us, "For you did not receive the spirit of bondage again to fear, but you received the Spirit of adoption by whom we cry out, 'Abba Father.' How tender is a father toward his children. He watches over us and protects us from danger and harm.

My daughter does not stop to ask for permission to approach me. She has had access to me from the day she was born. She just comes running up with a simple "Hi Dad!" and I stop whatever I am doing and turn my full attention on her and not only does she love it, she expects me to dote on her. Similarly, we expect God to care for us. It is so good to belong to the Lord. He has kept me from all evil. I am reminded that 1 Corinthians 6:19 says, I am "Not my own". In the Greek, it is "You are not your own property. You are bought with a price." The same way a king stamps his property with his seal of claim, the Lord has identified us as His own by placing the Holy Spirit in our hearts and we are sealed. Over these years, when I ran into trouble, I looked up toward heaven and called on His name. When He saw that I was in trouble, He came swiftly to my rescue.

It is good to belong to God. He gave us talents and gifts that we must use. We must not think that we will not be successful. Instead, we must stay focused and keep praying to God.

The enemy will try to discourage you and block you from doing what God has called you to do but he cannot stop you. Develop yourself and your talent. Whatever the Lord called you to do, get busy doing it. If you are a musician then you should practice daily – even if for only 5 minutes. My life has become better because after playing for these 40 years, I began to realize the importance of functioning in my calling. Don't let anything cause you to deviate from your calling. Work on whatever God has assigned you.

Many of us have escaped rigid religious backgrounds where we have been under the control of human traditions and church limitations. Renewal movements bring life, freedom and deliverance to us from religious bondage. But sometimes we are like children turned loose in a candy store--we become satisfied with power and zeal without understanding the responsibilities that accompany deliverance. God put the Church all together but man decided to take over. Though a lot of people left the Church, I stayed. All this time, God has been with me, looking out for me.

My values came by way of the Church of God of Prophecy. We should never give up on God's plan for us. If we will activate and use the gifts He gives us, the benefits will be astounding. For example, I have learned that whether being part of a band or playing an instrument, the experience will expand your knowledge of musical styles, genres and music history and help develop comprehension, communication, and social skills. Playing an instrument requires learning how to cooperate with others. Listening to music and playing a musical instrument stimulates your brain and can increase your memory and can refine listening skills. This has a long term effect. Other benefits of playing an instrument include self-esteem, perseverance, endurance under pressure, better eye contact and hand coordination, time management, organizational skills, discipline mastery and ultimately an appreciation for even the simple, and most boring musical notes.

As I played through my struggles, I experienced a lot of issues in the Church. I want pastors to know that they should stay in the presence of the Lord and keep on praising God. That is the only way you will be able to be the person that God called. I have seen too much wrongdoing from inconsiderate behavior to lying, stealing and mistreatment of the members. However the Bible warns against this in Ezekiel 34 where the word of the Lord came unto Ezekiel, saying, “Son of man, prophesy against the shepherds of Israel, prophesy, and say unto them, Thus saith the Lord God unto the shepherds; Woe be to the shepherds of Israel that do feed themselves! Should not the shepherds feed the flocks? Ye eat the fat, and ye clothe you with the wool, ye kill them that are fed: but ye feed not the flock. The diseased have ye not strengthened, neither have ye healed that which was sick, neither have ye bound up that which was broken, neither have ye brought again that which was driven away, neither have ye sought that which was lost; but with force and with cruelty have ye ruled them”.

He goes on to say, “My sheep wandered through all the mountains, and upon every high hill: yea, my flock was scattered upon all the face of the earth, and none did search or seek after them. Therefore, ye shepherds, hear the word of the Lord; As I live, saith the Lord God, surely because my flock became a prey, and my flock became meat to every beast of the field, because there was no shepherd, neither did my shepherds search for my flock, but the shepherds fed themselves, and fed not my flock; Therefore, O ye shepherds, hear the word of the Lord.”

In this passage, we get a clear picture of what is in store for leaders or pastors who mistreat the sheep.

Thus saith the Lord God; Behold, I am against the shepherds; and I will require my flock at their hand, and cause them to cease from feeding the flock; neither shall the shepherds feed themselves anymore; for I will deliver my flock from their mouth, that they may not be meat for them. For thus saith the Lord God; Behold, I, even I, will both search my sheep, and seek them out. As a shepherd seeketh out his flock in the day that he is among his sheep that are scattered; so will I seek out my sheep, and will deliver them out of all places where they have been scattered in the cloudy and dark day. And I will bring them out from the people, and gather them from the countries, and will bring them to their own land, and feed them upon the mountains of Israel by the rivers, and in all the inhabited places of the country. I will feed them in a good pasture, and upon the high mountains of Israel shall their fold be: there shall they lie in a good fold, and in a fat pasture shall they feed upon the mountains of Israel. And they were scattered, because there is no shepherd: and they became meat to all the beasts of the field, when they were scattered."

I don't know what A. J. Tomlinson, founder of the Church of God and the other faithful prophets intended, but the Church is still the Church. I have seen some wrongs that need to be corrected. I read where Tomlinson explained, "When I was sanctified my whole nature was changed, and my whole being was almost constantly going out after God." The Holiness way of life, with its emphasis on the Wesleyan doctrine of entire sanctification or "Christian Perfection," offered the former political activist an alternative ideology which led him to rearrange his priorities and interpret reality in a different way. Tomlinson's experience typified the effects of sanctification on many Church of God members. Economic hardship led them to join the church in search of a transcendent experience, but poverty alone did not determine who became a member of the church.

The talent, anointing, skills that were given to me to play the saxophone is undoubtedly a gift from God given to me so that His people may be blessed. If I could write my own epitaph, it would read, "He raised his Saxophone in Praise." The History books will have to tell it. It would be nice to go down in history as one of the best Gospel Saxophonists ever because I have such a fierce respect and appreciation for who the Lord is in my life. Nonetheless, if it doesn't make it to the history books, just let the world know this. He was a great man of God that feared and trusted God, and believed in His word. He was a loving husband, father, and family man. Most of all, let it be known that Ira Scatliffe really cared about helping people. His life set the example of how a child of God should live as a true believer in Christ.

An Interview

A Moment with Amos Carty, Jr. Esquire

Although we have now read the autobiographical sketch of Ira Scatliffe's young life, one never stops wondering whether there is more or if there is something more "candid" about our subject that we missed. It is quite possible to have "oodles of material" in your possible but never say anything worthwhile! Well, once in a while, an opportunity presents itself that you cannot pass up and you only have a very small window of time with which to prepare. Such is the case in this short simple interview. Sometimes these are the very interviews that are most insightful. Though was not conducted in person (as much as I would have liked to travel to the US Virgin Islands), I am happy to report that modern technology made the interview possible. Without further delay:

Welcome to the interview of a childhood friend: **Amos Carty, Jr., Esquire**

Foster. Most of us have certain memories that stand out in our minds over the years. Understanding your relationship to Ira Scatliffe, please share a couple of your earliest and fondest memories of him.
Amos. My earliest and fondest memories are of Ira and I talking in church and laughing at the quirky ways of certain church members.

Foster. That is interesting. Why do you think you have retained these particular memories of him?
Amos. These memories reflect who Ira is.

Foster. Did Ira have a nickname? If so, what was it?
Amos. Scat.

Foster. Well, that is apropos. I can see how the name is well earned from several perspectives. Between the two of you, who is considered

the wiser? Who is the oldest and by how many years are you separated?
Amos. Ira is four years older than me.

Foster. Close your eyes for a moment and think back to your childhood. Are you able to recall images of Ira as a little boy.
Amos. Since Ira is older than me, I do not recall him as a little boy.

Foster. How would you describe him? Was he a prankster? Funny? Obedient? Playful? Strong willed? Precocious? Always into something? Quiet? Studious? Happy? Talkative? Annoying?
Amos. He had a good sense of his humor.

Foster. In what ways is Ira still the same? In what ways has he changed?
Amos. Ira has not changed since our boyhood days and he still loves a good joke.

Foster. What characteristics or personality traits do you still see in him?
Amos. His humor.

Foster. Has he grown into the man you imagined or assumed he would become?
Amos. Yes, He has grown into the man I imagined him to be.

Foster. What has surprised you most concerning Ira's career path and why?
Amos. Nothing really has surprised me about Ira's career path.

Foster. What did you think about his decision to leave the Virgin Islands to live stateside?
Amos. It was a natural progression for Ira to leave the Virgin Islands.

Foster. Were you close friends? If so, how did that decision affect your friendship?
Amos. We still remained friends.

Foster. How did you remain in touch and correspond? How often?
Amos. We did not correspond that often until I went to America for college.

Foster. Was there ever anything that Ira did that made you (open-ended question) – please describe any or substitute others. Did he make you nervous? Uncomfortable? Cry?
Amos. No, but his jokes and humor made me laugh out loud.

Foster. Do you recall Ira ever sharing with you any hopes and desires for his life? Describe.

Amos. To be a world class saxophonist.

Foster. Ira seems to be quite confident. Describe a transparent moment. How did that enhance your opinion and / or respect for him?
Amos. I gained tremendous respect for him during the illness and subsequent passing of his sister, Naomi Scatliffe Donaldson.

Foster. There is usually a little twist to every life's story.
a. Were there any interesting twists to tales about Ira? Not that I can recall.
b. Did he always do what he said when he promised? Yes

Foster. What the most regrettable childhood memory you have of Ira?
Amos. I do not have any regrettable childhood memories of Ira.

Foster. What was the most teachable moment that you participated in?
Amos. I do not recall a specific teachable moment.

Foster. Here's the thing: Best friends are, well, the best. What do you feel is the single-most or greatest regret in life concerning Ira?
Amos. If there was anything I wish could have been done differently to prevent that moment or spare him, I would wish that he did not have to endure the loss of his sister.

Foster. Would Ira likely be different today if he had not experienced or gone through that situation? Or do you believe he would be the same?
Amos. Perhaps he may have been different. It made him stronger.

Foster. What was Ira "good" at in school – football, chess, basketball, drama, music? Do you recall when he started playing sax? What were your thoughts?
Amos. I thought he had the potential to be good.

Foster. When you first heard him play, what did you think? What was your reaction?
Amos. I thought he sounded good.

Foster. Did you ever dream he would "stick to it" all of these years?
Amos. Yes.

Foster. Knowing Ira as well as you do, use your imagination. If you had a chance to look at life through eyes of Ira, how would you answer these questions? What and how would you change the world?
Amos. I am unsure

Foster. What would life be like in public school's music department?
Amos. More resources for the students.

Foster. How would students with big dreams be treated?
Amos. Students with big dreams would be encouraged to pursue their dreams.

Foster. What did you disagree most on?
Amos. I do not recall us disagreeing on anything in particular.

Foster. Imagine you had the option to put two magic doors anywhere in the world for Ira. What's magical about these doors is that when you walk through one of them, you come right out the other, no matter how much physical distance is between them. Where would you put those doors for Ira, and why?
Amos. Ira wants to walk through the doorway to heaven to see his parents and sister.

Foster. If you could transfer all of your ability from one skill to that of another skill in order to approve the latter, which skill would you draw upon and give to Ira? What "skill" would you want him to improve? Why? How would it benefit him in his career?
Amos. I do not know of any skill I would give to Ira. He could improve on being less "cheap". His vehicle gas purchases would last longer.

Foster. If you had the option to receive a wall size, bigger than life picture depicting a single moment of Ira's future, at what point in his future would you like the photo taken, and why?
Amos. When he releases his first gospel album, a lifelong dream.

Foster. Finish the sentence, "There is nothing I would rather do for Ira than to ....
Amos. Finance his first album.

Foster. If you could swallow a pill that would stop something from happening to Ira again, what would the pill permanently end? Or if you could take a pill that would introduce a perfect scenario for Ira, what would be changed in his life for the better?
Amos. I am unsure.

Foster. What would you describe as the perfect place for Ira?
Amos. Any place with his wife, Julie and daughter, Jyrah.

Foster. Did you or anyone else ever play a prank on Ira? How did he handle it?
Amos. Yes. He was in "e flat". The rest is left to your imagination.

Foster. What was Ira's worst haircut you've ever seen (at any age)?
Amos. I do not recall.

Foster. If you could invite a famous person / people to dinner for Ira, who would you choose and why?
Amos. Najee since his professional hero, Grover Washington, Jr., died years ago.

Foster. Describe a real-life situation where you or Ira stood up for someone/something.
Amos. Against jewelry in the church.

Foster. Name an outlandish/wild thing you and Ira did – tell us about it.
Amos. Chase women in America.

Foster. What three things do you love about Ira?
Amos. His humor, loyalty and talent.

Foster. And three you could do without?
Amos. Nothing.

Foster. Share one bizarre encounter you had in life with Ira. How did it turn out?
Amos. I do not recall any bizarre encounters with Ira.

Foster. Share one thing about the world that you nor Ira understood about the world when you were a kid.
Amos. Nothing comes to mind.

Foster. Name something or someone you think Ira misses most from childhood?
Amos. His parents.

Foster. Tell me about the worst punishment you recall from Ira's child? Please describe what brought it about and how Ira handled it.
Amos. In Ira's own words, he was punished almost daily as a child's because he was disgusting.

Foster. If you could change one thing about his life, what would it be?
Amos. He would have several gospel albums.

Foster. What are some unusual hobbies that Ira had (or still has)?
Amos. Fixing old cars.

Foster. If you could choose an age that you could always be and hang out with Ira, what age would it be and why?
Amos. When we lived in DC. I have very fond memories of those days.

Foster. Did Ira ever cut class? Do you recall the circumstances?
Amos. I do not know. We did not go to school together.

Foster. When did you realize for the first time (If you can recall), that Ira had grown up? Describe that moment.
Amos. When he told me that he and Julie had gotten married. I was very proud of him. I was proud of them both when Jyrah was born.

Foster. If you were on a talk show and were asked an open-ended question to describe Ira S. What would you say? If you had one wish, what would it be?
Amos. An extremely humorous, loyal, talented, intelligent man who is one of my dearest and best friends.

Foster. If you had one wish one Ira, what would it be?
Amos. For him to be a famous gospel artist touching lives through the power of his spirit filled music.

Straight Talk:
A Little Talk with the Church

The music in a church is one of the most important areas of the Praise and Worship services. If your music is terrible (too loud, too ethnic, off key, out of whack, inconsiderate), visitors are not coming back. However, if you have a team of musicians who are worthy of their hire, then compensate them as appropriate. For many years now, many churches have not properly compensated their musicians but have demanded their loyalty, time, offering and service. Many musicians have been made to feel guilty and unworthy for not being able to participate in some functions. Some of them have become discouraged because they are treated wrongly while other staff members were compensated. The pressure for congregants to give is enormous so for the church that does not want to compensate a musician, here are a few comments.

Don't pay your musicians if you do not want your church to grow.

Don't pay your music department head if you do not want music organized and do not require a commitment that they will show up.

Do not compensate anyone if you don't want your attendance to double.

Do not pay the musicians if you don't want them to attend rehearsals.

Don't pay anyone if you don't want progression and want everything to remain outdated.

Don't pay musicians in the church if you don't professional quality sound.

Don't pay musicians if you want to put a demand on their schedules and want them to not feel insulted. There are a lot of costs involved: training, equipment, maintenance, production, gas and mileage. Surely, they may come to service anyway, but they do not always have their instrument packed and onboard.

If you pay people to clean the church, mow the lawn and answer the phone, then why not pay the staff musicians.

The Bible says "whatsoever ye do" do it in the name of the Lord. If the church budget can afford professional musicians, then pay them. We worship the Lord on our jobs, but it is still work. We worship in the office of administration and it is work. The pastor worships the Lord while He brings the sermon, but it is still work. If you don't believe it, check them out. Sometimes, they sweat. Sometimes they are very exhausted after. Sometimes, they stress over the workload. They preach and sometimes they are administrators so they have to make decisions concerning the church business. This is work people. Their doctor sometimes tells the pastor to take a vacation. Volunteers come and go as they please. I have even heard some pastors, from the pulpit, speak of firing their pastoral staff. If we appreciate our musicians, if their consistent participation is on demand or required by schedule, then we should establish a budget line item for them.

Special Tributes to Pastors and Overseers

From the Desk of Ira Scatliffe

Throughout the years of my music history, my life has been influenced by some truly great men and women of God. Recognizing the great sacrifices that our pastors, ministers and overseers have made and continue to experience, I have seized this opportunity to honor those special individuals that I admire and who have greatly impacted my life. I could not list everybody because of the sheer number. However, these are individuals that I consider the collective, earthly protection of my life from my youth to my present. Without their shining examples of love of the Lord, I would have given up long ago. May God bless these bulwarks, their memories, legacies, and families for all of eternity.

Ministry Capacity	Special Thanks and Appreciation
A.W. Carty, Sr., Pastor	It is important for me to express heartfelt appreciation for just how much his friendship, support and confidence in me has meant to me over the years starting from when I was only a teenager. He never put me down, but always believed in me and invited me to play my Saxophone before I reached adulthood. As I reached each milestone and became a professional, he continued to embrace my accomplishments.
Gloston Fahie, Pastor	This man of God believed in me before I became proficient on the Saxophone and yet saw me for what I would become. There were never any put downs and he always encouraged me to play solos. His warmth, courage and concern for others has always rang sincerely in everything he has done for me.

Kenneth Benjamin, Pastor	One of the most selfless people that I know who loved to hear me play and always wanted to seek opportunities for me to be heard among the people. His resourcefulness and support has always struck me as kingdom bound. It is people like this that confirms me and undergirds my desire to continue living for the Lord.
Aludus Todman, Pastor USVI Overseer	Encouraged me to play and promoted me, voluntarily seeking and providing many opportunities for me to play at conventions. My gratitude cannot be expressed sufficiently to characterize this level of support. He personally promoted me in ways that can only be surpassed by God.
Rufus R. Rogers, Overseer Verona Rogers (Minister)	He believed in me, wanting to hear me play; always speaking a good word, and helping me to get my foot in the door when I didn't have a leg to stand on. He and Sis. Verona have shown by example, the way to lead our lives and encourage others along the way as we continue to tread the roads of our journey. I will never forget them for the music they brought to the Virgin Islands and how they allowed God to use them in my life.
The Late Samuel R. Rhymer, Overseer	A strong father figure, his labor of love continues today. He loved for me to play with his sons, and always encouraged the bond between us. I will never forget the many hours we spent together, enjoying the presence of the Lord.
The Late Bishop George Jones	I will never forget how he counseled and guided me over the years. He was like an adopted father to me, listening and helping to solve my problems as though they were his. Whether they were about money, girls, car problems, I could tell him all of it. Like family, he took me under his wing. When in NY and pastor of the Church of God of Prophecy at various locations, he took me with him to revivals, concerts and programs, where I had opportunity to play Saxophone.
Bro. Joseph Gardner, Pastor	A wonderful inspiration and strong supporter, he had faith in me and encouraged me to produce a CD.
R.B. Finlayson, Sr. Overseer, Pastor	I believe God sent this General Field Secretary of the Church of God of Prophecy to the Virgin Islands

	just to get me started on the Saxophone. In many ways, he was my inspiration for the future before I even knew I had one. In addition to all he did for the Church of God of Prophecy in the Virgin Islands, he is known for being the kind of person who, when he walked into the room, he made you feel happy and grounded. He made everyone feel special.
Barney E. Trogdon, Overseer NY	He Believed in my playing. He saw me in the Assembly and personally called to express how proud he was to see me playing at the Assembly, Church of God of Prophecy, Cleveland, TN. This was the highest of honors for me as it gave me hope that such a serene icon, whose illuminating smile could light up the halls of Headquarters, would take the time out to uplift a young, upstart like me. His endorsement strengthened my inner man.
Adrian L. Varlack	He always encouraged me concerning my playing. Although I always amazed by the tremendous outpouring from other people, it is still encouraging for someone of his stature, a General Headquarters Representative from the Church of God of Prophecy, to pause for a moment to take a genuine interest in my future and pour into my life. It speaks volumes concerning this man's love for the Lord.
Albert Chatmon, Jr./Sr. Pastor	He always listens, instills confidence and sincerely respects me. He made me the Music Director of the New Beginnings Church of God of Prophecy and set me forth as a Deacon.
Howard Johnson	Likes to hear me play as evidenced by his happy smiles. Whenever I played, I would always find him standing somewhere in the back checking me out as he praised and worshiped the Lord. There is no better commendation or accolade than for the Almighty God to be lifted up as I play my Saxophone.

Made in the USA
San Bernardino, CA
05 June 2016